Quiltmaker's
Color Workshop

QUARRY

First published in the United States of America by

Quarry Books, a member of

Quayside Publishing Group

33 Commercial Street

Gloucester, Massachusetts 01930-5089

Telephone: (978) 282-9590

Fax: (978) 283-2742

www.rockpub.com

Library of Congress Cataloging-in-Publication Data available

ISBN 1-59253-276-4

10 9 8 7 6 5 4 3 2 1

Design: Laura Covallier, Laura Hermann Design

Cover images and photos on the following pages by Allan Penn: 135, 137 (top), 145 (top), 148 (top), 151 (top), 154 (top)

Printed in Singapore

Quiltmaker's
Color Workshop

GLOUCESTER MASSACHUSETTS

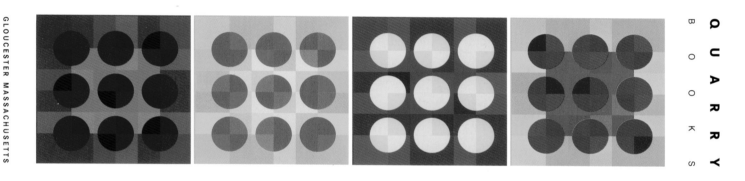

QUARRY BOOKS

FUNQUILTS' GUIDE TO UNDERSTANDING
COLOR AND CHOOSING FABRICS

Weeks Ringle and Bill Kerr

CONTENTS

Quilt Projects

INTRODUCTION

Life is such a wonderful teacher. When we published this book in its original edition, we had no idea how it would be received. We knew readers would love the impressive array of quilts from our contributors, but we weren't sure if they would understand our approach to color selection. Rather than suggesting that quiltmakers choose theme fabrics and companion fabrics to match, we suggest they develop an idea, and then choose a palette that expresses the idea. There are no fast and easy formulas for good color choices; only thought, experience, and a willingness to try many options.

In the three years since the original edition was published, we have been delighted by the feedback we've gotten. We've received emails such as the one from a watercolorist in Germany telling us that the book is being used as a textbook for a painting class. Knitters have written to say that it has been helpful with yarn selection.

From our work with quilters worldwide we have also learned a great deal more about the difficulties people face in choosing colors for their quilts. With calls and emails from Denmark to New Zealand, we have been reminded that selecting colors is quite challenging, and the more tools people have to help them with their selections, the easier it is.

So, when our publisher approached us about the reissuing of *Color Harmony for Quilts*, we saw it as an opportunity to include a workbook section that would provide step-by-step suggestions for understanding color and selecting fabrics. We have added four original patterns that teach various color principles, along with a checklist of questions and tips, which can be photocopied and taken with you to the fabric store. To demystify the design process, we included a case study that shows how we selected and eliminated fabrics for one of these new quilts. In this case study, we explain that learning how to "edit" fabric by removing the ones that don't work is as important as figuring out which ones do work.

Color theory is complex, and most books on the subject are written for painters. This book seeks to provide the basics of color theory as it pertains to quiltmaking. We examine how talented quilters whose styles range from traditional to contemporary have used innovative color combinations and great ideas to create inspirational quilts. By honing your analytical skills, you can learn to see color in a new way and use color to reinforce an idea in a quilt. This book is not about learning how to figure out which colors "go together," but rather determining which colors effectively and beautifully express an idea.

Most important of all, you will come to understand that there are no magic formulas for using color in quilts. There are no foolproof methods. Good color work, like good design, comes from exploring—being willing to try different combinations before settling on a final palette. It is all part of the design process, which is highly personal and varies greatly from quilter to quilter. We hope this new edition encourages even more quiltmakers to explore color options in every quilt they make. Be fearless; it's only fabric.

HOW TO USE THIS BOOK

Quiltmaker's Color Workshop is a guide to thinking about color in a new way. We want to show you how some of the great traditional and contemporary quiltmakers use color in their designs. You will learn the basics of color theory, but because we are dealing with fabric, not paint, we will also explain how the subtleties found in various types of fabric can either improve or detract from your palette. Our intent is not to tell you which colors match and which don't, but rather to expose you to successful palettes used to express the design intentions of great quilts. This book will help you talk about color and develop the analytical tools needed to select colors and fabrics with confidence.

The book opens with a practical approach to color theory. Color inspiration comes from many sources, not just the shelves of fabric in your favorite quilt shop. The book encourages you to appreciate color in quilts as well as in the world around you. This section includes definitions of terms used when discussing color. There is also a general discussion of fabric—understanding, purchasing, and organizing a collection of fabric, commonly known among quilters as a "stash."

The second section contains fifteen chapters, each based on a palette and a quilt demonstrating that palette. Some of these quilts are traditional, some are contemporary. What they share is noteworthy color work from which everyone can learn. We have included an artist's statement to let the artist explain his or her use of color in the quilt. Each quilt is described in terms of palette, the color wheel, and proportions of colors used. An analysis of the relationship between the color and the overall quilt

design follows. Every chapter includes abundant illustrations applying that palette and variations of it to one of the following quilt patterns: Log Cabin, Sawtooth Star, Drunkard's Path, Wild Goose Chase, and Thousand Pyramids.

All of the fifteen chapters finish with a workshop page of explorations for individuals and groups. Each exploration encourages you to experiment with and talk about color. Of particular note are the exercises for groups. The social aspect of quilting is an important one. Getting a group of friends or a guild together for these explorations not only increases the fun of experimenting, but also gives quilters the opportunity to learn from each other.

The Gallery section of the book shows quilts whose color work was chosen to inspire you. Each includes a brief statement by the artist.

The last section is a workbook that will help you apply the color theories you've read about in the previous sections to the quilts that you make. The workbook includes four patterns from the FunQuilts studio. Each pattern will help you develop a different skill in working with color. We think the most challenging aspect of choosing fabrics is developing a palette comprising multicolored prints. This is the type of palette used in our Zanzibar quilt. We decided to use this quilt as a case study, taking you through each step of the decision-making process. It's useful to understand the "Big Idea" behind the quilt and to see which fabrics we included. It's equally helpful to see which fabrics we didn't include and why. Often it's the fabric "editing" process that is the most challenging.

COLOR THEORY

Color and the Big Idea

While most quilters have, as one student put it, "more fabric than I could possibly use in my life-time," many settle on a palette for a new quilt too quickly. When beginning a new quilt, it is tempting to approach it like a recipe: flip through a book, find a pattern, go to a quilt shop, and purchase a specified amount of fabric. While color in and of itself is seductive, it is best used in support of a larger design intention. In other words, think of a great idea first, then figure out how color will help express the idea. The big idea, as we call it, does not have to be a heavy intellectual statement. It can be playful or quite simple. Inspiration for original designs can come from something as simple as a child's swingset in the backyard to a breath-taking vista seen on a family vacation. If you take the time to think about your idea and use color in support of it, you'll end up with a quilt that is very much your quilt. If you can't sum-marize your idea in a sentence, you probably have too many ideas or one that has not been fully developed.

Our *Pink Lemonade* quilt (see Gallery, page 129 and above) explores the change in color that happens when ice is added to a glass of pink lemonade on a hot summer day. As the ice floats to the top of the glass, a full spectrum of pink appears, ranging from darkest pink at the bottom of the glass to the luminous light pink seen through the ice at the top. Starting with a big idea helped us determine the colors as well as the design of the quilt. Had we added any other colors to the composition, they would have detracted from gentleness of the pink.

Color and Meaning

Many people think of color as being universal; that yellow is the same in the United States as it is in Japan. In fact, color has layers of both cultural meaning and regional significance. While yellow is associated with cowardice in the United States, it symbolizes grace and nobility in Japan. In Asia, white is often associ-ated with death. Think of the other ways that color has become associated with certain ideas such as the scarlet letter of shame, the red menace of communism, green environmental-ism, and the purple heart for courage.

Just as colors have meaning in every culture, every region of the world has a certain palette of colors that can be found throughout its environment, architecture, textiles, and art. Often, these colors relate to natural elements found in the region. The Mediterranean region is home to brightly colored flora not found in colder lands. There, housing materials and col-ors are designed to reflect the sun rather than absorb it. In the same way that a turquoise and pink house might look cheery and bright in a sunny beach setting, it would look garish in a sophisticated London neighborhood. If you are creating a quilt that is about your vacation to a Central American rainforest or are designing a quilt that is about growing up in your home-town, color can enrich the meaning of the quilt.

Color Theory

COLOR TERMINOLOGY

Learning about color theory through examples makes it manageable. The more one learns about color, the more complex it seems; so it is important to define the words we use to discuss color. While people disagree on whether a certain fabric is blue-green or green-blue, knowing the following words will be helpful in the discussion of color in this book and in general.

HUE is what most people mean when they say "color." It is the general term for the colors on a simple color wheel. Red is a different hue than blue (see figure 1).

VALUE is the degree of lightness or darkness of a hue. These reds are the same hue but one is a lighter value than the other (see figure 2).

SATURATION is the intensity of a color and is relative to the hue and value. Fully saturated colors appear brighter and clearer while less-saturated colors appear either more milky or more gray. A fully saturated yellow has a much lighter value than a fully saturated blue (see figure 3).

PRIMARY COLORS refer to the three basic colors that when combined make all other colors. Red, blue, and yellow are primary colors.

SECONDARY COLORS refer to the combinations of equal amounts of two primaries. Violet, green, and orange are secondary colors.

COMPLEMENTARY COLORS refer to colors that are across from each other on the color wheel (see figure 4).

ANALOGOUS COLORS are those that appear next to each other on the color wheel (see figure 5).

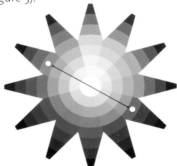

figure 4—COMPLEMENTARY

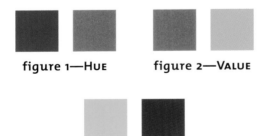

figure 1—HUE   figure 2—VALUE

figure 3—SATURATION

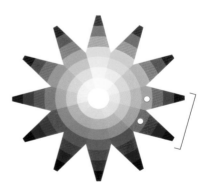

figure 5—ANALOGOUS

THE COLOR WHEEL

Color wheels range from those that include just the three basic primaries and three secondaries to those that include nearly every color in the rainbow. A color wheel that includes at least a dozen hues and a variety of values is most useful in analyzing the palettes used in quilts. We have added a gray scale to the bottom of the color wheel so that we can represent grays and black, often important elements of a quilt. As part of the analysis of the quilts in the next section, the colors appearing in the quilt will be indicated on the color wheel and gray scale with small white dots. Many quilts have hundreds of subtle hues and values, so we have used the dots to indicate the general palette, not the exact hue or value of each color. With such a color wheel, you will see how some of the palettes discussed in this book are predominantly one value with multiple hues, while others are mixed values and mixed hues (see figure 6). For an in-depth discussion of color theory, nothing beats Johannes Itten's seminal work *The Art of Color*.

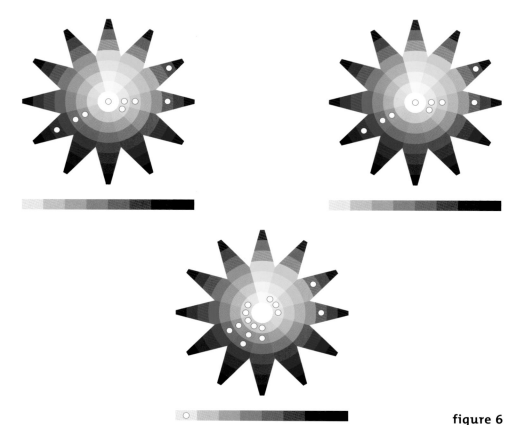

figure 6

USING COLOR

Successful Palettes: Letting Go of "Matchioso"

Contrary to popular belief, a successful palette is not one in which everything necessarily "matches." In fact, palettes that match too perfectly often result in predictable quilts lacking in depth. Many fabric manufacturers and quilt shop clerks suggest that the novice quilter begin a quilt with a multicolored theme fabric and then choose the other fabrics by using other colors found in the theme fabric. Some fabric manufacturers even develop what they refer to as companion fabrics to reassure the quilter that fabric A can be used with fabric B. We refer to this approach as "matchioso." While this approach minimizes the risk of ending up with fabrics that clash, it discourages the quilter from exploring new palettes and creates a formulaic palette that is neither original nor supportive of a larger design intention. And some would argue that it takes a lot of fun and adventure out of making a quilt.

Differentiating the *Role* of Color from Color Itself

Isolating and analyzing the colors found in an inspirational quilt forces the viewer to reevaluate which colors really go together and why. Another surprise found in analyzing the palettes of great quilts is that there are often fabrics in a quilt that one would dismiss as ugly, muddy, or boring when seen on the bolt in a fabric shop. But it is often these fabrics that can transform an otherwise boring collection of colors. Consider in the quilt below how the addition of this mustard transforms an otherwise predictable grouping into a more dynamic one.

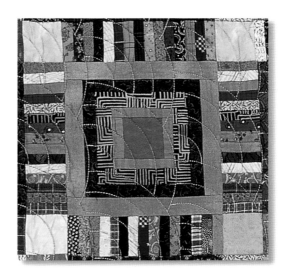

color theory

Everything's Relative

The power of a given color is based on the context in which it's seen—it is relative to its surroundings. Think of the way a chef garnishes food. A red cherry might be a beautiful garnish for a piece of coconut cake as the small bit of red makes the white of the coconut seem even whiter. The white of the cake makes the red of the cherry seem even brighter. Imagine the same red cherry atop a bowl of strawberries. The cherry almost disappears, blending in with the red strawberries. This is why chefs will choose a garnish that is a complementary color to contrast with the food, making both appear more vivid. The best garnish for the bowl of strawberries would be a vivid green mint leaf, which would show both the red and the green to their best advantage. Some garnishes may be more subtle: shavings of dark chocolate atop a bowl of coffee ice cream may enrich its appeal.

In the same way, variation in hue, value, or saturation can create depth when used with subtlety. The *Raindrops* quilt (shown at right) is about the delicacy of raindrops. The subtle shifts in value and hue reinforce the delicate nature of water. The soft grays, blues, and lavenders evoke an image of a quiet, cloudy, misty morning. The same design would be far less compelling with dark navy mixed in with the softer blues and grays. The contrast of value and saturation would be too jarring. Similarly, breaking away from the analogous palette would also provide too much contrast for the big idea of raindrops; a complementary color such as red or orange would disrupt the soft, quiet feel of the quilt.

Rethinking Proportion

In a quilt shop, all of the bolts are the same size, and you see each color and fabric in equal amounts. It is hard to remember that each color will be used in varying amounts. In the same way that one does not add in equal amounts flour, sugar, and salt to a batch of cookies, evaluate the role of each color in your design before determining how much of it to use. For example, a predominantly orange palette might look even more cheery with a slim 1/2" (1 cm) binding in complementary celery green (see figure 7), while a quilt of equal amounts of saturated orange and green will appear loud (see figure 8). Using fabrics in different quantities can add dimension to a quilt. When working on a nine-patch, take the time to think about how the overall quilt might change if there were some hierarchy to the proportion of colors included rather than cutting equal numbers of each color. Is one fabric more dominant than another? Using less of a dominant color can make a quilt gentler while using more of it might make the quilt bolder.

figure 7

figure 8

Have No Fear...It's Only Yellow

The use of yellow has long been controversial among quilters. Some claim that one should restrain the use of yellow to "less than 7 percent of the quilt" lest one end up with a yellow quilt. While it is true that some colors will take over a quilt when used in large amounts, this danger is not limited strictly to yellow. Rather, it is a balance between the hue, value, and saturation used in a palette. The phobia over yellow has lasted so long that there are generally few choices for yellow in the marketplace. The inclusion of yellow is not appropriate for every quilt, but it is the most overlooked color in the quilting world, and there are many palettes that would be improved with the addition of yellow. Look how important the role of yellow is in each of these images (right and opposite).

Finding Inspiration for Color

When developing a palette to support your big idea, search for inspiration before you set out to buy fabric. Surveying the natural environment can reveal subtle colors in prairie grasses along the highway, lichen found on trees in the woods, wildflowers along streambeds, moss on garden stones. Animals are also wonderful sources of color inspiration. Birds, frogs, horses, and insects vary from region to region and offer surprising color combinations.

In addition to nature, there are beautiful color combinations to be found in art museums—analyze a painting you like: how many different colors do you see?—and natural history museums: how did different cultures combine colors in gemstones or clothing?

Photography is also another great source for interesting color work. Flip through *National Geographic* to see how some of the world's best photographers use color in their compositions. Collins Publishers' *A Day in the Life* series shows how dozens of different photographers have captured the essence of a country. Look at the relationship between colors in the photograph. How do the colors reinforce the scene captured in the image? Spend a few minutes at the library looking at books on graphic design, architecture, and interior design. Items found in daily life, such as cereal boxes, toothpaste tubes, and magazines, also use color to communicate ideas. By understanding the relationship between an idea and the color used to express it, you will not be limited to duplicating other people's palettes but be free to develop your own.

BLOCKS AND FABRICS

Choosing a Quilt Block and Fabric to Reinforce Your Big Idea

As noted before, each aspect of the quilt should work to reinforce your design intention. Think of this as a mission statement for your quilt. Compare the *Raindrops* quilt and the *Pink Lemonade* quilt (see pages 24 and 129). The intention of the *Raindrops* quilt was to capture the delicate quality of rain. The rounded edges of the traditional Mill Wheel block reinforced the idea of drops of water. Using a Pineapple block, with its many sharp corners, would have totally changed the feeling of the quilt, even if the color palette remained the same. Look also at the quilting pattern. The swirling stitches of the drops contrasts with the flat stippling on the field. Note how the pieced binding provides a smooth transition to the edge of the quilt rather than a severe frame. Think also about how using printed fabrics instead of solids would change the quilt. Printed fabrics have at least two different colors of different hues and or values printed on them. Prints inherently have more visual depth than solids. In the *Raindrops* quilt, visual flatness and subtlety were an important part of trying to capture the quality of rain; therefore, we chose to use solids.

Conversely, the *Pink Lemonade* quilt was designed to capture the value fade that occurs when ice is floating in a glass of pink lemonade. To ensure a smooth flow from pink to white, patterned fabrics and the simplest of piecing patterns were essential. Seams needed to disappear to make the fade convincing. Tiny, 1" (3 cm) squares create the smoothest transition.

There are times when you may just want the experience of making a traditional quilt using a certain fabric. In this case, it's best to work backward. What is it about that fabric or that block that is so engaging? If it's a simple block such as Broken Dishes or a Nine Patch, palettes with minimal contrast, in hue and value, will work as well as those with greater contrast. If contrast is important to your design, be sure to choose colors and fabrics that can be differentiated from a distance of 15 feet (4.6 m) or so. As a general rule, it's a good idea to stack up all of the fabrics selected for a quilt and look at them from across the room. Printed patterns can look radically different from 2 feet (61 cm) away than they will at 15 feet (4.6 m). If there's a fabric that stands out or "pops," reevaluate whether or not it's serving the desired role in the composition. If there is insufficient contrast between pieces in a complex block, the overall quilt may seem poorly defined or muddy. Too much contrast might appear severe.

PRINTS VS. SOLIDS

Solid fabrics have all but disappeared from the local quilt shop. It is increasingly hard to find a broad selection despite their small, loyal following. Solids are useful for abstract or subtle designs; prints are generally preferable for designs that call for more richness or visual depth. Although there are quilters who mix prints and solids, it is hard to do successfully because it tends to make either the solids or

prints stand out. If you are making a quilt with prints and need a green square, a monochromatic, green-on-green print is probably a better choice than a solid. If you are afraid to use only solids in a quilt for fear of it becoming boring, you should review the tradition of rich, dynamic Amish quilts, all of which were made with solids.

MIXING SCALES IN PRINT FABRIC

When using printed fabrics, the scale of the pattern and the size of the repeat are critical to executing a well-designed quilt. Many blocks can handle large-scale prints, but a 2" (5 cm) square may look very different cut from one area of a large-scale print with a 20" (51 cm) repeat than from another area of the same fabric. When using a large-scale pattern or repeat, cut a few samples before committing to the fabric for the entire quilt. Used carefully, a combination of large-scale and small-scale prints in the same quilt may create more visual interest and depth than sticking to one or the other, but analyze how the pieces are going to work together before investing in hours of cutting.

MULTICOLORED PRINTS

Multicolored prints are often marketed as "theme" fabrics by fabric manufacturers or quilt shops. These beautifully printed fabrics often beg to be purchased. There is a temptation to use them with other less attention-grabbing fabrics such as monochromatic prints that match colors found in the theme fabric (refer to the earlier section on "Matchioso," page 11, for more on this topic). While this approach is sometimes successful, it often results in a formulaic, one-dimensional quilt. A more interesting approach is to scour your stash and your fabric store for other multicolored prints that can hold their own against the first theme fabric. Quilters are often shy about using more than one multicolored print in a quilt for fear of the quilt becoming too busy. But there are instances in which adding more multicolored prints mutes the dominance of a single one while adding a rich variety of color. One trick to using multiple, multicolored fabrics is to limit the range of values of the prints. For example, use a variety of dark to medium value multicolored prints. Another way to prevent a collection of multicolored prints from overwhelming a quilt is to use them with a simple design. As a general rule of thumb, a complex palette flatters a simple design, and a simple palette is best suited to a complex design.

USING FABRICS WITH WHITE

White is perhaps the trickiest member of any given palette. As it contrasts sharply with any hues with medium to dark values, it can stand out. Even the smallest of white flecks in a navy pattern can really make a fabric "pop" from a distance. White can be used in any quilt if it enhances the design intention of the quilt rather than undermines it, but it is often best suited to medium and lighter value palettes. When working with fabrics that contain white, periodically view your work from a distance to confirm that the white is not calling too much attention to itself.

THINKING AHEAD: BACKING, BINDING, AND QUILTING

It's a good idea to determine which fabrics will be used for the backing and binding before starting a quilt. Nothing is more frustrating than having a finished quilt top and being unable to find an appropriate backing or binding fabric. The decision about the binding and backing may also influence which fabrics are critical to the quilt top. Think about the quilting thread as well. Should it stand out or disappear into the palette established in the quilt top? It is always tempting to want to think about these details later, but they are important color and design choices that influence the success of the quilt.

Guidelines for Buying Quilting Fabric

THE VIRTUES OF COTTON

Without exception, the best fabric for functional quilts is 100 percent cotton. Traditionally, crazy quilts were made with silks and velvets, but most people will find that keeping silks and velvets clean when used every day is a chore one can live happily without. For wall hangings and art quilts, anything goes as long as you are aware of the durability and characteristics of the materials. The average quilter who may have pets or children and plans to have the quilt on a bed or as a throw on the back of a sofa will appreciate the washability and durability of cotton.

CHOOSING AND USING FABRICS

Although the number of quilt designs is unlimited, most quilters are limited by the fabrics available commercially. Many quilters experiment with dyeing their own fabrics, but printing a complex twelve-color print is not an option. There are three general categories of quilting fabric found in most quilt shops: solids, prints, and hand-dyed fabrics.

SOLIDS are fabrics that have been completely immersed in, or printed with, one color of dye.

PRINTS are fabrics that have been printed with as few as two or as many as a dozen or more different dyes to achieve a repeating pattern.

HAND-DYED FABRICS can be solid colors or have an irregular, mottled coloration of one or more colors. They are usually made in small batches so it is difficult if not impossible to find two hand-dyed fabrics that are identical. Included in this category are batiks that feature simple, often crudely printed patterns created with a wax-resist method. The color and precision in batiks is generally more mottled and less consistent than that found in prints. Although some fabrics labeled as batiks are actually printed to simulate batiks, the manufacturing process is less of interest here than the appearance of the fabric in the context of a finished quilt.

SOLID

PRINT

HAND-DYED FABRIC

CHECKING THE QUALITY: WHAT'S WORTH $10/YARD AND WHAT ISN'T

When buying fabric, cost cannot be overlooked. National retailers boast large selections of $3/yd (1 m) fabrics. Fabrics at quilt shops generally average $6-10/yd (1 m). Is this price difference a reflection of volume discounting or of quality? When trying to gauge the quality of a fabric, it's useful to understand a bit about the economics of the manufacturing process. Manufacturers have lines of fabrics that are aimed at certain segments of the quilting market. Some are marketed to the bargain shopper, others are marketed to quilters seeking heirloom-quality fabrics.

Manufacturers that aim for the bargain market reduce their costs by doing any or all of the following things: buying a lower-quality, loosely-woven, cotton base fabric; using lower-quality dyes; using less-sophisticated printing machines; using fewer dyes; and using designs that require less printing precision.

Manufacturers who market to heirloom-quality quilt makers generally start with a tighter weave of higher quality cotton; richer, more durable inks; more precise printing processes; and they tend to hire the best fabric designers. So, how do you tell them apart?

First, feel the fabric. Compare it to other fabrics in the store at different price points. A stiffer fabric usually indicates a poor quality of printing or that the fabric has been overdyed Overdyeing will cause problems with wear and washing as uneven fading may occur as early as the first wash. A tightly woven cotton with more threads per inch will wear better than a more loosely woven cotton. Hold an expensive fabric from a quilt shop up to the light next to a bargain fabric from a national chain. Can you see a difference in the density of the weave? When you find high-quality fabrics, note their manufacturers and keep track of those whose fabrics wear well. Most manufacturers' fabrics are even in quality across their product lines.

Second, look at the printing of the fabric. Is the pattern crisp or does the pattern look a bit blurry? Blurriness is a sign that the various colors in the fabrics have not been aligned precisely in the printing process. This is known as poor registration. The edges along the length of a bolt of fabric are known as the selvages. In most cases, but not always, prints will have a white stripe down the selvage with the manufacturer's name, the line of fabric, and the name of the designer printed on it. Sometimes there is also a series of color dots on the selvage. These dots are samples of the dyes used in the printing of that fabric. As a general rule, each time the manufacturer adds another dye to the production process, the cost of the fabric increases. Manufacturers of low-end fabrics rarely use more than two or three dyes. That is not to say, however, that two-color prints are necessarily of poor quality. There are many makers of two-color prints of excellent quality. If there are four or more colors on the selvage, prepare to pay more for that fabric. Most of these fabrics are printed on high-quality fabric.

Most national fabric chains carry mostly bargain-quality to midrange quality fabrics. In contrast, most quilting shops carry only mid-range to high-end fabrics. Remember, the time and energy it takes to make a quilt far outweighs the cost of fabric. When putting together a stash of fabric, opt for quality over quantity. Options for reducing the cost of buying fabric include setting up a fabric swap within a guild, checking bargains on the Internet, and asking local quilt shops about preinventory sales.

A WORD OF WARNING

Be cautious if using vintage fabrics. Although you may be delighted to find calico prints from the 30s in your Aunt Louise's attic, realize they may not wear well. Being decades old, they may be deteriorating. The phrase "they don't make them like they used to" may not be such a bad thing. Some older cottons were crudely woven or printed with dyes that shortened the lifespan of the fabric, so before investing hours in a quilt using your vintage find, think twice. Fortunately, there is a wide selection of reproduction fabrics available that bring the designs of past eras to the modern manufacturing processes of today.

Finally, be careful if buying the "same" color from two different bolts. If the fabrics were not dyed or printed in the same batch they may not be identical. Most fabric shops order just one bolt at a time, and their inventory may move slowly, so when they reorder it may be six months later and the fabric may be from a different batch.

To Wash or Not to Wash

There is great disagreement among quilters about whether or not to prewash fabric prior to quilting. And if so, what sort of soap should you use? Harriet Hargraves has written extensively on this subject, and we recommend her book *From Fiber to Fabric*. Many quilters will opt for the equine shampoo recommended by Hargraves, while others will rely on a readily available gentle soap such as baby shampoo. Regardless of your stance on soap, we believe prewashing fabric is always a good idea. First and foremost, this is a health issue. You will be breathing in the fibers from cutting the fabric without knowing what chemicals might be on the fabric. What sort of chemicals and dyes were used in the printing and finishing of the quilt? While chemicals are regulated in this country, many fabrics are printed abroad where no such controls are in place. Perhaps the bolt was placed on the floor of the shop the day the exterminator came through spraying insecticide along the baseboards of the factory. Do yourself, your lungs, your skin, and your immune system a favor: Prewash all fabrics before adding them to your stash. If the health reasons aren't compelling enough, prewashing will determine whether or not the fabric will bleed, and preshrinking it before use will eliminate first-wash jitters once the quilt is completed.

Keep It Organized

Whether your workspace consists of your kitchen table or a well-appointed studio, keeping fabric organized and readily available is critical. Depending on the size of your stash, organize the fabrics by hue into boxes with lids to keep out dust and light. While plastic is not desirable for long-term storage of quilts or fabric because it limits air flow, it's fine for quilters who are using their fabric regularly. Try to fold the fabric into a uniform dimension so all of the pieces can be viewed at once, much like books on a bookshelf. Consider dedicating one box to multicolored prints that have no dominant color. Arranging a fabric swap with friends is a great way to clear out fabrics that are no longer useful and gain some new fabrics. Otherwise, set aside fabrics you no longer like for a charity project. The less visual clutter in your stash, the more clearly you'll be able to see which fabrics are available for your next project. Smaller scraps (less than 4" × 4" or 10 cm × 10 cm) can be sorted by hue in boxes for scrap projects or charm quilts.

SUBTLE

Raindrops has a calming influence on the viewer. The clear colors, solid fabrics, and large-scale blocks minimize visual distractions. The dominant blues and greens evoke water while the composition of the circles mimics falling rain on a pond. Traditionally, the Millstone block, on which Raindrops is based, is used in 4"– 6" (10–15 cm) blocks, but here each block is a full 12" (30 cm) square. With its graphic composition and confident color work, Raindrops reads well at a distance and rewards the viewer with textural detail of the quilting up close.

RAINDROPS

36" × 48" (91 cm × 122 cm)
Weeks Ringle and Bill Kerr
of FunQuilts
1999
Cotton fabric and batting
Machine pieced and
machine quilted

Artists' Statement: "Raindrops is an exploration of color and form designed to express the subtlety with which rain falls in a pond. To add depth to the design, the palette is limited to creams, grays, and analogous greens, blues, and lavenders in light to medium values. Subtle value and hue contrasts reinforce the delicate nature of rain and a sense of layering. The circles appear to be on a different plane from the background. The large scale of the blocks highlights the purity of color and the simplicity of the inspiration for the design."

Subtle Palette

ORIGINAL PALETTE—SUBTLE

Most pastel palettes rely solely on muted colors of low value and saturation while *Raindrops* adds medium values to bring unexpected, but not startling, contrast. Starting with pale cream, the palette ranges to much darker blues and greens, a range larger than standard pastel palettes. Gentle blues and greens dominate the quilt, but the cream, light gray, and pale lavender provide variation and complexity. The soothing feel of the palette comes from the limited range of hues. Any reds or oranges would generate too much contrast.

Color Wheel

The hues in *Raindrops* span from the tiniest hint of yellow found in the cream to the violet of the pale lavender. Most of the colors are concentrated in the range of analogous blues and greens. Although the cream and violet are complementary colors, they are so desaturated that the effect is harmonious.

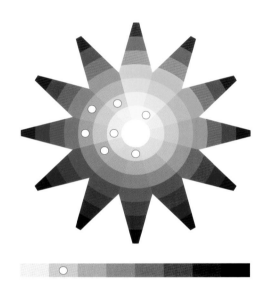

Proportion

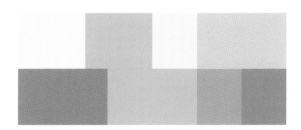

Raindrops contains an even balance of light and medium values, but remains dynamic by having an uneven number of blocks of each hue.

Analysis

In *Raindrops*, color is used to emphasize the idea of subtle contrast. The contrast of hue and value described earlier reinforces the contrasts of form: square and circle. These forms are further differentiated by the quilting; the squares are stippled while the circles are quilted in free-hand spirals. This quilt demonstrates how value is relative. On a dark background the quarter circle of pale lavender appears light while on the light cream background it appears darker.

Note that the binding of the quilt incorporates random size pieces from each of the fabrics. With the simplicity and spareness of the design, this border accentuates the color work.

Palette Variations

**ORIGINAL PALETTE
SUBTLE**

Subtlety is created by small, regular increments in difference among hues and values. The original Subtle palette moves evenly from light values to medium values—when used in equal proportions, no one color dominates. These variations show how changing either the breadth of the palette or the increments within it dramatically alter the feel. The Drunkard's Path block has contrasting curved and straight pieces with well-defined edges. Note how this contrast of forms responds to the changes in the palette.

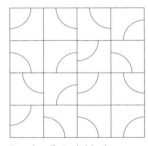

Drunkard's Path block

Variation 1
Minimizing the value contrasts maximizes the hue differences.

Variation 2
Using only light values minimizes the value contrasts, creating a gentle palette.

Variation 3
Paring down the palette to just four colors emphasizes their differences.

Applying the Palettes to the Drunkard's Path Block

VARIATIONS IN HUE

ORIGINAL PALETTE—SUBTLE

Variation 1

Variation 2

Variation 3

subtle

Applying the Palettes to the Drunkard's Path Block

VARIATIONS IN VALUE

VARIATIONS IN PROPORTION

Color Workshop: Understanding Value

Determining differences in value can be a challenge. Some quilters have stashes of fabric that are dominated by one value, maybe it's predominantly lights or darks. Sometimes this is by choice and sometimes it is by oversight. Introducing new values into your stash may change the complexity of your future quilts.

INDIVIDUAL EXPLORATION

Pull out your entire stash of one hue—all of your reds, for example. Create a value scale by arranging the fabrics from lightest to darkest. Are the gradations between different values somewhat consistent? Do you have lots of darks and mediums, but no lights? Looking at the fabrics from across the room might help you spot gaps. If you spot gaps, consider buying even a quarter of a yard of the missing value to supplement your stash.

GROUP EXPLORATION

Each member of the group should cut two 2" (5 cm) squares from each of five predominantly blue fabrics. Create two piles and have everyone put one square of each fabric in each pile. Now divide into two teams. Each team will take one pile and arrange the squares in a line, making a value scale from light to dark. Once both teams have finished, compare the two lines and discuss any differences. At the end of the session, each team can draw straws to see who gets to take the whole collection home!

BEYOND THE QUILT

Go to a hardware store and collect paint chips of all the whites. Cut them up into individual squares, and try to figure out where each would fall on the color wheel. Is there a hint of red or blue in that white? Find the "purest" white on the sheet. Hold it next to the others. Among all of the yellowish whites (commonly referred to as creams or naturals), are there value differences or just hue differences? Remember how different whites can be when you next use white in a new quilt.

subtle

EXOTIC

This quilt is reminiscent of the heavenly portrayals found in Chinese paintings and on traditional Chinese porcelains. The palette is limited to just a few hues, as any more would distract from the complexity of the composition. Color supports the big idea in this quilt. The big idea here is a view of traditional Chinese life, its stories and myths. Limiting the palette to colors found in traditional Chinese art makes the portrayal more convincing.

OLD CHINA

58" × 86" (147 cm × 218 cm)
Chadidjah Alsegaf
1997
*Cotton fabric and
polyester batting*
*Machine appliquéd
and machine quilted*

Artist's Statement: "This quilt was inspired by the traditional motifs of the fabrics. The main design of the quilt is an old tree, a symbol of longevity and a productive life. The dragon is a powerful, mythical creature that symbolizes all the good things that happen in one's life: protection, prosperity, and fertility."

Exotic Palette

ORIGINAL PALETTE—EXOTIC

The palette features the shade of orange-red associated with Chinese architecture and dragons. The complementary blues remind the viewer of the sky as well as traditional ceramics. The addition of the browns defines the tree around which tiny figures meditate, dance, and play with animals. The dark blues, browns, and blacks at the bottom of the quilt anchor the composition and prevent the massive dragon at the top of the quilt from overwhelming the piece.

Color Wheel

The reds are made even more vibrant by pairing them with several shades of blue. The rich browns found in the tree trunk are repeated in the smaller forms of the monkeys and deer, offsetting the brilliance of the orange-reds. Similarly, the pale blues and whites offer value contrast, providing a backdrop for the many figures.

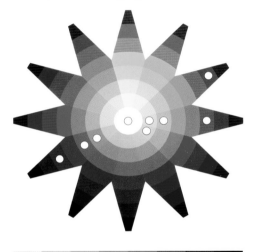

Proportion

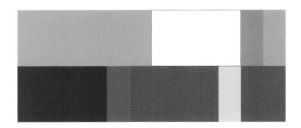

Although the reds comprise less than a quarter of the quilt, their saturation and lacy use in the composition make them appear more abundant. Similarly, the prominent placement of the dark brown makes it appear larger. The pale blues and whites appear in equal amounts, providing respite from the highly detailed composition.

Analysis

Some quilts are all about color. This quilt is a good example of the appropriateness of certain colors to a given subject. The role of color in this quilt is to support the composition and make it convincing. Had the artist used green, a literal and common color used to portray trees, the entire quilt would have lost its Chinese quality. The unusual use of colors is also compatible with the dreamlike quality of the piece. The colors and the composition do not attempt to replicate reality but, rather, create a dream of an exotic land.

Palette Variations

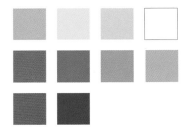

**ORIGINAL PALETTE
EXOTIC**

The Exotic palette demonstrates how color supports the big idea of a quilt. When separated from the design of the *Old China* quilt and shown as color swatches, the palette retains an Asian feel. But when it and its variations are applied to a traditional American Log Cabin block, they appear unexpected but not necessarily Asian.

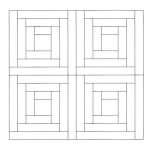

Log Cabin block

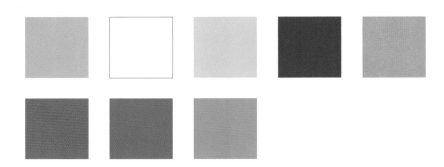

Variation 1
Removing the tan-orange hues makes the palette more graphic.

Variation 2
Soft violets can be added to the base colors making it less Asian but still exotic and unexpected.

Variation 3
Removing the lightest values lends a bolder feel to the hues.

Applying the Palettes to the Log Cabin Block

VARIATIONS IN HUE

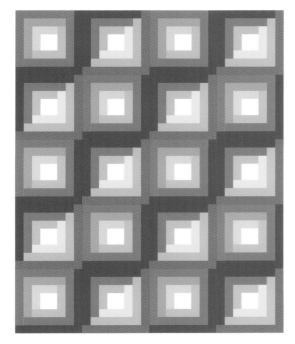

ORIGINAL PALETTE—EXOTIC

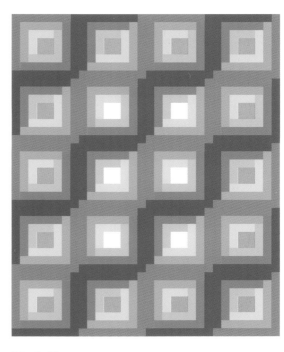

Variation 1

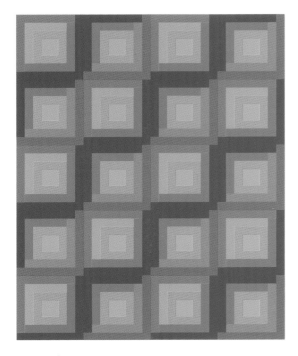

Variation 2

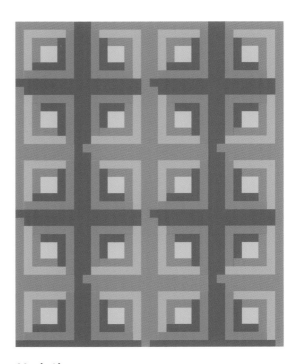

Variation 3

exotic

Applying the Palettes to the Log Cabin Block

VARIATIONS IN VALUE

 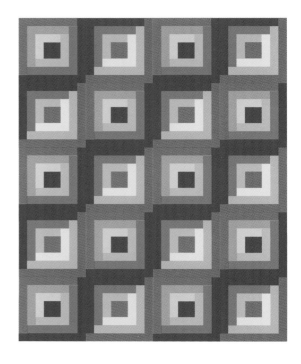

VARIATIONS IN PROPORTION

 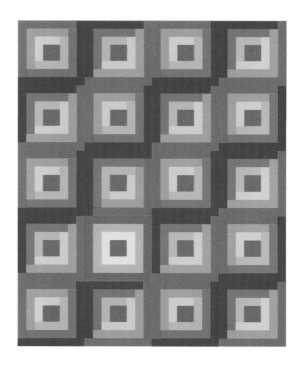

Color Workshop:
Color and Culture

Every area of a country has its own palette defined by the natural features of the region and the culture that has developed there. Often, it is hard to notice things to which we have become accustomed. The explorations below are designed to help you hone your skills of observation and provide an opportunity to become more in touch with the palette unique to your region. You are likely to find a wealth of color ideas right in your own backyard.

INDIVIDUAL EXPLORATION

Think about the region in which you live. Evaluate the amount and intensity of the sunlight you get and how it changes with the seasons. Look at the colors of old buildings in your town. Are they brick? Stone? Painted? How about the flora and fauna? Is the landscape primarily agricultural, urban, suburban?

Keep a "color calendar" for two weeks. Each day when you're out of the house, try to spot a color that occurs commonly in your region. Snip a small square of fabric that is close to the color you noted. At the end of the two weeks, look at the palette you've accumulated. Is it an accurate representation of your area? What's missing? Think about how that palette would be different if you lived in a different region of your country.

BEYOND THE QUILT

Check out a world almanac from your local library if you don't have one at home. Look at the flags of the world. Each country chooses colors for the flag based on their own history and culture. The almanac should explain the meanings of the colors in each flag. Note how each country interprets the meanings of a color differently.

GROUP EXPLORATION

Have each person in the group develop a block using a palette that reminds them of a special place. It could be a favorite vacation spot, an often-visited picnic spot, or hometown. When each person is done, have other members try to guess the location the quilter had in mind.

exotic

RADIANT

October not only evokes the colors of the season but captures the flow of seasonal change and the complexity of autumn colors. The quilt attracts the eye to areas of rich color then draws it across the composition to explore the wide range of colors and forms. *October* acknowledges the richness of detail, contrast, and color of nature.

OCTOBER

42" × 31" (107 cm × 79 cm)
Catherine Kleeman
2000

Commercial and hand-dyed cotton fabric, cotton batting, decorative threads
Raw edge machine appliquéd, machine quilted, bobbin stitched

Artist's Statement: "The inspiration for *October* was autumn colors—reds, oranges, yellows, with bits of green and brown. I selected fabrics in various shades of these colors, both commercial and hand-dyed pieces. I then made many, many circle-on-square blocks, always keeping in mind the color combinations and how I wanted color to appear in the quilt. Next, starting with a blank design wall, I began placing blocks, rearranging as necessary, until I was pleased with the composition. The most exciting part of the process is creating the design, and it's the part I enjoy most. The end result is always a surprise."

Radiant Palette

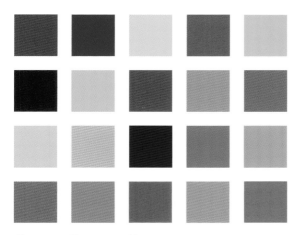

ORIGINAL PALETTE—RADIANT

The palette is predominantly reds and oranges with complementary hues of greens with yellows, blues, and browns appearing throughout the quilt. Most of the colors are highly saturated and, with the exception of the light oranges and greens, they are medium to dark in value. Occasional glimpses of light and dark values add depth to the piece.

Color Wheel

The use of highly saturated, complementary colors makes this a bold palette. Using a broad value spectrum of greens and reds modulates the tone of the quilt, preventing it from becoming brash. The mottling of the hand-dyed fabrics also softens the contrast between the complementary hues and values.

Proportion

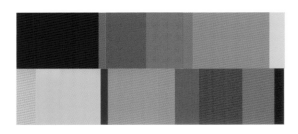

The quilt uses even amounts of reds and greens, but because the reds and analogous oranges and yellows are more saturated than the greens, the reds and oranges appear dominant.

Analysis

This quilt is a wonderful example of contrasts— some bold, some subtle. The contrast of the circles within the squares is more evident in some squares than others. Some of the circles have minimal hue and value contrast compared with the squares upon which they are appliquéd. Other circles are in bold contrast in value and/or hue to the squares on which they are sewn. It is the varying of contrasts that makes some of the squares visually recede while others seem to be moving toward the viewer.

radiant

Palette Variations

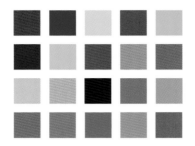

**ORIGINAL PALETTE
RADIANT**

The brown tones lower the volume of this palette. When they are eliminated, the palette is vibrant and more graphic. Simplifying the palette by either relying only on analogous colors or fewer value contrasts reduces the radiant quality seen in the original palette.

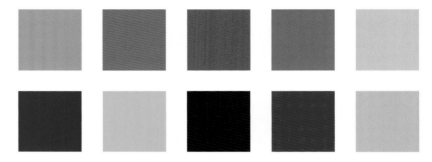

Variation 1
Removing the browns makes the palette brighter.

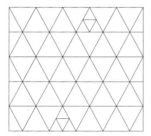

Thousand Pyramids pattern

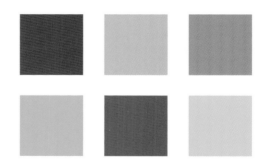

Variation 2
Without the blues, the palette is quite hot.

Variation 3
The blue and green contrast sharply with the rest of the palette, which is predominantly red.

Applying the Palettes to the Thousand Pyramids Pattern

VARIATIONS IN HUE

ORIGINAL PALETTE—RADIANT

Variation 1

Variation 2

Variation 3

radiant

Applying the Palettes to the Thousand Pyramids Pattern

VARIATIONS IN VALUE

VARIATIONS IN PROPORTION

Color Workshop:
How Directors Use Color

Filmmakers, like quilters, are very aware of the importance of color and light. They use color to set the mood for a scene, define a character, symbolize good or evil, represent an era, or set the tone for the whole movie. Becoming more aware of the power of color can help you gain confidence in selecting colors for your next quilt.

INDIVIDUAL EXPLORATION

Rent one of your favorite movies, get yourself comfortable, and have your stash nearby. As the movie unfolds, pull out fabrics that mirror the colors used in the movie—either literally in the costumes or sets or as an abstraction such as through mood or lighting. By the end of the film, you should have quite a palette piled up. Does it evoke the feel of the movie? If not, add or subtract fabrics until the palette suggests the tone of the movie.

GROUP EXPLORATION

Get together with your stashes, a TV, and VCR. Rent a movie that uses color in interesting ways—some suggestions would include *Gone with the Wind*, *Dick Tracy*, *The Sound of Music*, *Batman*, *Out of Africa*, and *Witness*. As the movie unfolds, each person should pull out fabrics that mirror the colors used in the movie. By the end of the film, each of you will have assembled a palette that is your interpretation of the movie. Compare palettes and talk about how color was used in the film. Don't forget to make popcorn.

BEYOND THE QUILT

Go to a movie and think about the colors used. Take note of how the strength of color is much greater on the large screen than on a small-screen television. If you have a college or university nearby that offers a film study class, consider taking it. The professor will be sure to discuss the use of light and color, which should get you thinking in new ways about your quilting.

COSMOPOLITAN

Sunlight on Flowers is a reminder of how even the most humble solid fabrics can be transformed into a sophisticated and timeless quilt when the colorwork and composition are masterfully designed and executed. This quilt relies on elegant hue and value contrasts to create patterns. The absence of patterned fabrics reinforces the quilt's crisp, graphic appeal.

SUNLIGHT ON FLOWERS

70" × 57" (178 cm × 145 cm)
Heather W. Tewell
1999

Cotton fabric, cotton batting, cotton thread
Machine pieced, hand appliquéd, and hand quilted

Artist's Statement: "My favorite way to work with color is to let my eyes be filled with it from studying the subject in nature. I often take photographs to see more, not to have an accurate palette to reproduce. When I select fabrics (the photographs put away), I visualize every nuance of color ... hue, intensity, value ... that I can remember. Working from memory allows me great freedom. For this piece, I studied a planting of poppies. I chose a complementary color scheme to intensify the reds."

Cosmopolitan Palette

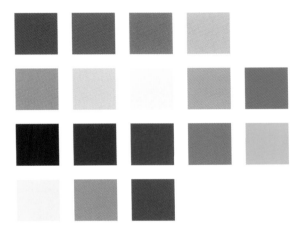

ORIGINAL PALETTE—COSMOPOLITAN

This palette comprises a variety of hues, values, and levels of saturation. Although the colorwork appears bold, its boldness is achieved not through bright, highly saturated colors, but rather, through contrast. A thin, yellow line on an olive green square makes the green seem bright, but when the same olive is used with a pale blue line, it seems more muted. The playfulness of both the colorwork and patchwork makes the palette seem even broader than it actually is.

Proportion

This quilt comprises predominantly medium to dark values of reds, blues, greens, browns, oranges, and grays. Although light-value hues make up only a quarter of the palette, the massing of the predominantly pale squares into two long columns makes it appear that the lights and the darks are nearly even in distribution.

Color Wheel

Note the range of hues and values as seen on the color wheel. Although there are many pairs of complementary colors used in the palette, some are more subtle than others. Of particular note are the complementary pairings among the lightest values. Look at the pale blues next to the pale peach tones for an example of how even the softest, most muted colors are strengthened by using complementary colors adjacent to them. Very few of the colors in the palette are fully saturated, "pure" colors. Note how much gray or yellow is in some of the greens and how much orange is in some of the browns. Although individually some of these colors might be considered "muddy," the combination of them together appears quite clear.

Analysis

This quilt is a good reminder of balance. Note how the thin strips of light fabrics make the dark blocks appear less dominant while the big, chunky squares set inside the lighter ones make them seem more substantial. Much like *Raindrops* on page 24, this quilt shows how value can be relative. Note how the medium blue looks so light next to the darker blue but so dark next to the palest blue.

Palette Variations

ORIGINAL PALETTE
COSMOPOLITAN

Most of the hues in the original palette are represented in three values: light, medium, and dark, but with subtle color shifts from value to value. The Sawtooth Star block allows for different readings especially when paired with the range of hue and value contrasts found in these palette variations.

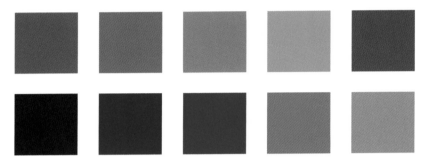

Variation 1
Removing the light values flattens the quilt while retaining the richness of the wide range of hues.

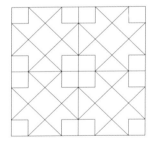

Sawtooth Star block

Variation 2
Using one hue from this palette in greater proportion will make it seem even stronger than colors that are more saturated or darker.

Variation 3
Limiting the palette to medium values will soften a quilt even if the palette includes complements.

Applying the Palettes to the Sawtooth Star Block

VARIATIONS IN HUE

ORIGINAL PALETTE—COSMOPOLITAN

Variation 1

Variation 2

Variation 3

Applying the Palettes to the Sawtooth Star Block

VARIATIONS IN VALUE

VARIATIONS IN PROPORTION

Color Workshop: Communicating Color

We all perceive and name colors differently. What you might call rust, your friend might call pumpkin. Our color vocabularies vary—some people think of colors as limited to the big box of crayons they had as a child, others may be passionate about color and be able to name hundreds with little effort. These explorations are to practice naming and describing colors.

INDIVIDUAL EXPLORATION

Make a list of every color you can possibly name, such as ruby, safflower, turquoise, ochre. Once you think you've got them all down, think about the origin of these color names. Put check marks next to your favorite colors. Do they have anything in common? Are most of them the bright colors of flowers or subtle earth tones? Are they evocative of a favorite place or time in your life? Do these colors continue to inspire you or is it time to try a totally new palette?

GROUP EXPLORATION

Divide into groups of no more than four people. Using only solids and monochromatic prints, one person will cut six 2" (5 cm) squares of different-colored fabrics, keeping the choices hidden from the group, and glue the squares in a row on a piece of paper. Without showing anyone the fabrics, the chooser will describe each of the colors in sequence to the group. If the description is, "The first square is a dark blue, like a fresh blueberry," the people in the group will each find a corresponding blue in their stash that they will cut out and glue on a piece of paper. Next might be, "To the right of the blueberry-blue is a brown that is just a bit lighter in value than the blue, like coffee with just a splash of milk added." The others would then add that color to each of their rows. The leader continues until the entire row of colors has been described. Then, compare each person's row to the leader's original. Repeat this exploration with each member of the group taking a turn as leader.

BEYOND THE QUILT

Subtle variations of color abound. The first step to learning to describe and work with colors is to take the time to notice them. A good way to do this is to start a collection of similar objects and pay attention to their differences. If you have a jar of pennies, spread them out and sort them by value or hue. Some are light, some dark, some are very orange, others brown, and some are even tinged with green tarnish. For a week, each time you go out, pick up a small rock or pebble from your yard, the road, a streambed, or a parking lot. Once you've collected twenty stones, spread them out and look at their colors. How would you describe them? How would you sort them?

QUIET

Equivalents whispers the message that value and hue contrast need not be bold to be successful. This quilt is all about being soft spoken but having a clear message. Some of its edges are soft and muted while others are clearly defined. This gentle palette of analogous, light to medium colors is a wonderful foil to the bold geometric forms of the circles and diamonds in the block. Note how the restrained use of these pale colors produces a quilt that is strong in form but gentle in color.

EQUIVALENTS

82" × 82" (208 cm × 208 cm)
Rebecca Rohrkaste
1999
Cotton fabrics and cotton batting
Machine pieced and machine quilted

Artist's Statement: "In this version of the Moon over the Mountain block, I planned to use earthy, atmospheric, low-contrast colors, taking advantage of the hand-dyed fabrics I'd purchased combined with mostly subdued printed and solid fabrics. Warm colors predominate with the cool turquoise and blues subordinate. There is a nearly full spectrum of color (favoring tertiaries)—not pure hues but many tints, tones, and shades. I introduced more value contrast as I proceeded to increase the oomph, yet retain the softness and the atmospherics.

I don't work from a color formula but from an initial idea or feeling and from the fabrics I have; from what I see 'working,' or not, as I design with the fabrics, within the pattern I'm using, and its proportions and the size of the finished quilt. And always with the awareness of the interactions of value, color, and patterns."

Quiet Palette

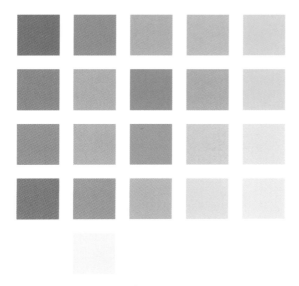

ORIGINAL PALETTE—QUIET

This palette redefines the conventional notions of pastels and their associations with baby quilts. The addition of beiges and medium browns to pastel blues, grays, and lavenders changes the perception of the palette into one more reminiscent of mist and fog than of a baby's first quilt or Sun Bonnet Sue.

Proportion

In terms of value, about one-third of this quilt would be considered whites or creams with another third as lights or pastels. The medium tones complete the palette. There appears to be a relatively even distribution of lavenders and creams with a smaller proportion of blues and beiges. Note how the darkest fabrics adjacent to much lighter fabrics allow the pieces of the block to read crisply.

Color Wheel

On the color wheel, this palette appears quite limited. It is, however, the subtle value differences between the fabrics that make the palette appear to have many more colors than are represented on a basic color wheel. This quilt is an excellent example of how limiting a palette to a small range of hues and values enables the eye to differentiate each color in more detail.

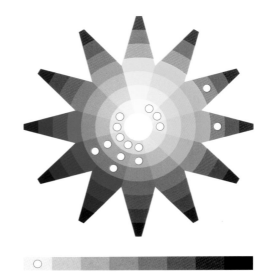

Analysis

Restraint is an undervalued quality among quilters. It is so easy in a store with four thousand bolts of fabric to gravitate toward the most vibrant colors. Most of the fabrics in this quilt would not beckon you from across the store but wait quietly on the shelves. There lies the lesson. It is in the combination of fabrics that great colorwork occurs, not in having one great fabric that dominates all others. This is color harmony.

Palette Variations

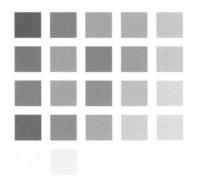

ORIGINAL PALETTE
QUIET

When the hue and value differences in a palette are minimal, any changes, however slight, are dramatic. Applied to the Thousand Pyramids pattern, these palettes create very different quilts—some with depth, some that are flat.

Variation 1
Removing some of the light to medium tones reduces the contrast and depth of the palette.

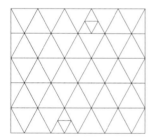

Thousand Pyramids pattern

Variation 2
Simplifying the palette to analogous hues amplifies the differences in value among the remaining colors.

Variation 3
Without the lights, the triangles appear to blend into one another, resulting in a softer, flatter composition.

Applying the Palettes to the Thousand Pyramids Pattern

VARIATIONS IN HUE

ORIGINAL PALETTE—QUIET

Variation 1

Variation 2

Variation 3

quiet

Applying the Palettes to the Thousand Pyramids Pattern

VARIATIONS IN VALUE

VARIATIONS IN PROPORTION

Color Workshops:
Color and Mood

Music can create moods. So can color. These explorations will help you think about how color can represent the mood set by a piece of music. In the same way that dancers and figure skaters interpret the mood of a piece of music, so too can visual artists such as quilters.

INDIVIDUAL EXPLORATION

Choose a piece of music from your collection or borrow one from your local library. Opt for music without words or one with words in a foreign language that you don't understand. Look for music that has a definitive mood—happy, tragic, reverent, mysterious, euphoric, tranquil. Something unfamiliar is ideal as you have no associations with it that might influence your color selection. If you're looking for somewhere to start, consider "Chan Chan" by the Buena Vista Social Club, "The Main Title Theme" from *The Last Emperor* soundtrack, any of the Gregorian chants featured on *Chant* by the Benedictine Monks of Santo Domingo de Silos, "Take the 'A' Train" recorded by Duke Ellington and his orchestra, "Epilogue" by Bill Evans, any of the African tribal chants included on *Deep Forest*, or *Zydeco Boogaloo* by Buckwheat Zydeco.

Place your stash and your sound system within reach. First play a piece of music and just listen. Then play it again. While it's playing the second time, start pulling fabrics out that evoke the music. Play the piece several times, introducing or eliminating fabrics until you feel as though you have a representative palette. If you were to design a quilt block that captures the spirit of the music, what would it look like? Think about any of your favorite pieces of music. Would they be useful in developing a palette? Next time you hear a piece of new music, think about what "color" it would be.

GROUP EXPLORATION

Choose a few of the previously listed pieces of music. Schedule a day when the group can do the prior exploration with three different pieces of music. Have a show-and-tell. Discuss why each person made the color choices they did. Consider making blocks from the palettes derived from each recording. Piece the blocks from the same music together to create a quilt to be raffled as a fundraiser for a local school's music or art program.

BEYOND THE QUILT

Attend a live performance of music or theater. This can be anything from a child's piano recital to an opera. While the music is playing or the drama unfolding, imagine that you have been hired to create a promotional poster of the performance. Which colors would you use to convey the mood and spirit of the performance?

quiet

VIVID

Bauhaus demonstrates that great quilts can be made from the simplest of forms and techniques, as long as the colorwork is focused. The sharp contrast between blocks is heightened by the use of complementary colors and the use of solid fabrics. The graphic composition of form and color sets a bold and confident tone.

BAUHAUS

40" × 80" (102 cm × 203 cm)
Sushma Patel-Bould
2002

Cotton fabric and batting
Commercial cotton fabrics
double layered to increase
saturation of colors and
minimize showthrough
Machine pieced and
machine quilted

Artist's Statement: "The *Bauhaus* quilt is an experiment with the principle of color interaction. The design is a tribute to our female ancestors who evolved the art form of woven textiles by embracing technology and modern production methods in service of bringing the beauty of handcrafted arts to many. The palette is inspired by the vibrant color harmonies of nature. The dynamic hues of earth and sky contrast and balance with the precise geometric composition of this machine-quilted textile. The bold color fields and delicately veiled quilting lines create an optical mixture that transforms the warp and weft of the front and back into a unified and harmonious whole."

Vivid Palette

ORIGINAL PALETTE—VIVID

This palette is all about contrasts, both in hue and value. The oranges are complements to the greens. The stark white is in sharp value opposition to the forest green. The saturation of the bright yellow and bold orange are also in contrast to the pale green, beige, olive green, and rust. These muted colors are critical in preventing the palette from becoming too severe.

Proportion

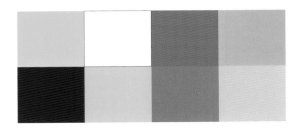

Although each of the colors in the palette is used in nearly equal amounts, the greens appear to dominate. The eye groups the light green, olive green, and dark green together and sees them as somewhat similar. Likewise, the rust and the orange reinforce each other, appearing more abundant. White appears to be used the least because all of the other colors have darker values.

Color Wheel

The dots on the color wheel show the sharp contrasts in hue and value of this palette. Although only eight different fabrics are used in this palette, the differences in both hue and value make the palette seem larger than it is.

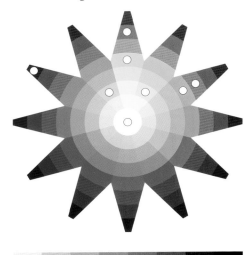

Analysis

Compare the placement of the white dots on the color wheel of this quilt with the color wheel analysis for *Raindrops* found on page 24. While the *Raindrops* palette is about subtle contrast, this palette is about bold contrast. Note also how the stark white in *Bauhaus* makes the entire quilt seem crisper while the cream in *Raindrops* softens the rest of the palette.

Note how the large swaths of color also increase the boldness of this quilt. Smaller pieces would have detracted from the boldness of the palette, while larger pieces would have made the quilt overpowering and static. This is a great example of balancing color, scale, and proportion.

vivid

55

Palette Variations

The strongest element in a palette is that which contrasts most with the rest of the palette—whether in hue or value. These variations show how the relative strength of one color can be perceived differently depending on the makeup of the rest of the palette.

ORIGINAL PALETTE
VIVID

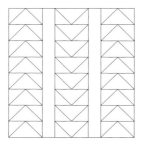

Wild Goose Chase block

Variation 1
While the bright yellow was the strongest single element in the original palette, removing it makes the dark green appear more dominant.

Variation 2
With minimal hue and value differences in this palette, all the colors seem harmonious.

Variation 3
The saturated orange appears even stronger with the contrast of this otherwise sedate palette.

Applying the Palettes to the Wild Goose Chase Block

VARIATIONS IN HUE

ORIGINAL PALETTE—VIVID

Variation 1

Variation 2

Variation 3

Applying the Palettes to the Wild Goose Chase Block

VARIATIONS IN VALUE

VARIATIONS IN PROPORTION

Color Workshop:
Crossing the Color Wheel

Working with complementary colors can be challenging. This exploration will help you use complementary colors to either turn up or turn down the volume of your quilt.

INDIVIDUAL EXPLORATION

Go to your dresser and open a drawer. What's the dominant color of the first piece of clothing you see? Find a piece of fabric in your stash that most closely resembles that color. Find its place on the color wheel then look directly across the color wheel to find its complementary hue. Think about how different the two hues would look together in lighter and darker values. Develop a palette of six to twelve colors that incorporates these two complementary colors. Investigate how incorporating a range of values changes the perception of the palette.

BEYOND THE QUILT

Advertisers often use complementary colors and value contrast to grab the attention of shoppers in supermarkets. Complementary colors are frequently used in detergent packaging to make them seem strong and powerful, while personal care products—such as shampoos and soap—tend to have soft, analogous palettes, making them seem more gentle. Food is carefully packaged to make it appealing. The next time you're in a supermarket, take note of the palettes used in packaging.

GROUP EXPLORATION

Have everyone place a 2 1/2" (6 cm) square of any fabric into a grab bag. Have each member pull out a square without looking. Each person will then look through their stash for a fabric that is the complement of the one they chose. Using the chosen square, its complement, as well as any other fabrics needed to create an interesting palette, develop a 6" × 6" (15 cm × 15 cm) block (finished size). When creating this palette, think of an adjective that sets the tone for the palette.

Have a show-and-tell of the finished blocks. See if the group can guess the adjective each person had in mind.

vivid

VIVACIOUS

I'm Bloomin' Again has a lot to say. Incorporating virtually every hue on the color wheel, this quilt asks the viewer to take in every stitch of its loveliness. The clear, vivid hues and forms of the flowers contrast with the dark greens used as the field on which the flowers are set. Note how the green field becomes lighter around the paler flowers, not only creating a sense of sunlight, but ensuring that the contrast between the field and the flowers is not too severe.

I'M BLOOMIN' AGAIN

86" × 90" (218 cm × 229 cm)
Ann Trotter
1997
Cotton fabric and batting
Paper pieced, machine quilted

Artist's Statement: "This quilt was designed using nature's color palette from my flower garden. Each flower was pieced using a color that would occur naturally for that species. I wanted the quilt to look like the sun was shining in the center, so I started with darker shades on the outer edges, becoming progressively brighter toward the middle."

Vivacious Palette

ORIGINAL PALETTE—VIVACIOUS

This palette concentrates on the most-saturated hues on the color wheel. Although the field of greens ranges from dark to medium in hue, the flowers are predominantly medium to light in value. Note that complementary colors are used adjacently—blues next to oranges, purple pansies with yellow centers, deep reds used on rich greens—making the colors appear even more saturated and rich.

Proportion

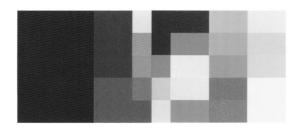

The various greens dominate the palette, yet because their value is darker than that of the flowers, the greens tend to recede into the background of the quilt, allowing the lighter and brighter colors to come forward and appear more dominant.

Color Wheel

This palette is a good example of how the deepest saturation of each hue can be found at different value points on the color wheel. A fully saturated yellow is of a lighter value than a fully saturated blue or violet. Note how the white dots fall in many different values around the wheel as would be expected in a quilt that is about not only color but sunlight and shadow.

Analysis

There are hundreds of different fabrics used in this quilt. In any great quilt with a lot of colors and even more printed fabrics, there has to be one central, organizing element that prevents it from becoming chaotic. The decision, conscious or not, in this quilt was to differentiate the values between the field and the flowers. Had the values been the same, the quilt would have appeared flat, lacking the depth achieved here. Similar values would also have made it difficult to perceive the forms of the flowers.

Palette Variations

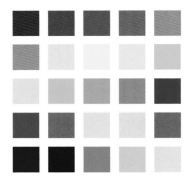

ORIGINAL PALETTE
VIVACIOUS

These palettes and quilt variations are good studies in proportion. When each color is used in equal proportions, the palette seems much brighter. In the original quilt, the composition was dominated by dark green. Substituting other hues or using the original hue in smaller amounts results in a much brighter palette.

Variation 1
This palette relies on the medium and light tones as the darks have been eliminated, creating a gentle mood.

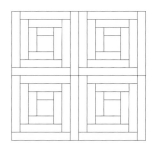

Log Cabin block

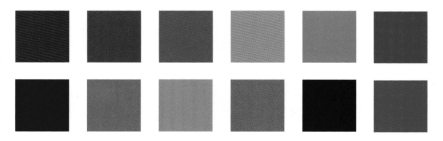

Variation 2
In contrast, this palette adds the darks and eliminates the lights to create a more dramatic mood.

Variation 3
Saturated yellow appears strong in a palette of fewer colors. Placing the bright yellows of this palette into the quilt in a grid, rather than randomly, also tones down the overall "volume" of the quilt.

Applying the Palettes to the Log Cabin Block

VARIATIONS IN HUE

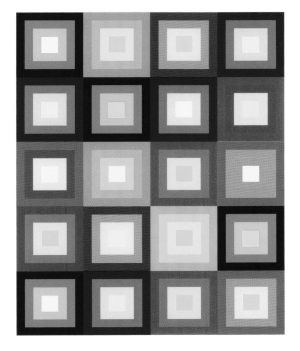

ORIGINAL PALETTE—VIVACIOUS

Variation 1

Variation 2

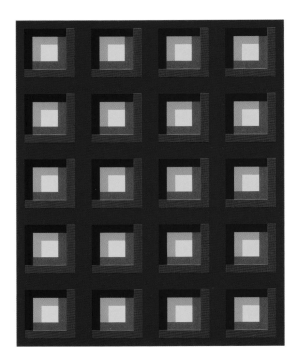

Variation 3

Applying the Palettes to the Log Cabin Block

VARIATIONS IN VALUE

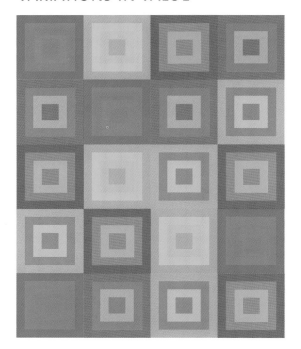 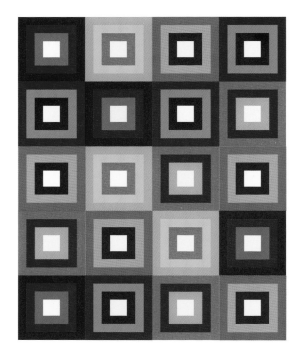

VARIATIONS IN PROPORTION

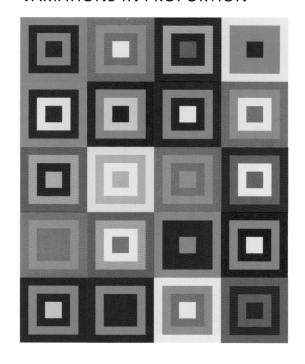 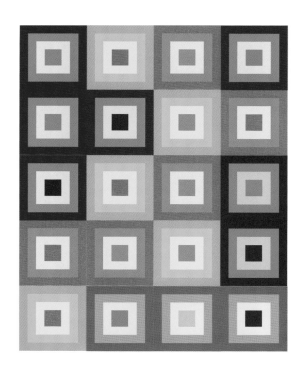

Color Workshop:
Changing Light

Fluctuations in daylight change the way we perceive colors in nature. Taking note of how colors in your environment appear to change throughout the day can help you understand the association of certain colors with certain times of day. Fine tuning your awareness of light will help you develop rich and sophisticated palettes for your quilts.

INDIVIDUAL EXPLORATION

Choose a sunny day when you'll be home all day long. Choose a colorful, stationary object to keep track of throughout the day. It could be a tree, a window box, or a parked car. Make sure that direct sunlight hits it at some point during the day. At 7 A.M., noon, 5 P.M., and 7 P.M., take note as to how the colors change. Notice how the noonday sun can cast harsh light that may make the object appear more washed out. What hues and values are most noticeable in the morning light and the late day sun?

BEYOND THE QUILT

Claude Monet loved to paint the same scene at different times of day. For inspiration, go to the public library and check out some books that include his time-sequence paintings of haystacks or the Rouen cathedral. Evaluate how Monet made each painting so evocative of a particular time of day.

GROUP EXPLORATION

Figure out how many hours of daylight there are at the time of year when you're planning the project. Divide up the amount of daylight by the number of people participating. For example, if there are twelve hours of daylight and six people participating, each person would get two hours of light. Write the intervals of light on slips of paper— 7 A.M.–9 A.M., 9 A.M.–11 A.M., 11 A.M.–1 P.M., and so on. Place in a grab bag. Each person then makes a 6" × 6" (15 cm × 15 cm) (finished size) crazy quilt block that best represents that time of day.

When finished, line up the blocks according to the assigned time, and discuss how each person made their color decisions.

MYSTERIOUS

When we first saw Gloria's quilt, she explained her thinking about color by saying, "Black is a bright." Many quilters hesitate to use black in a quilt for fear of it making the whole quilt seem dark and dreary. *Study in Browns* is an excellent example of how black can make other colors appear richer and more dramatic. The inspired use of creams and yellows in conjunction with the blacks and dark browns give this quilt a mysterious quality.

STUDY IN BROWNS

67" × 86" (170 cm × 218 cm)
Gloria Spaete
2000

*Cotton fabric and
polyester/cotton batting*

*Machine pieced,
machine quilted and
machine trapunto*

Artist's Statement: "I love color! I want my quilts to look like rich oil paintings saturated with color. I take risks to achieve the color I want. My favorite quilt store in Madison, Wisconsin, had a fabulous collection of browns. After admiring them for many months, I finally broke down and took an eighth of a yard of each one home with me. I chose a simple pattern and made up blocks with a wide range of values, adding rusts, blacks, and light values as the quilt evolved."

Mysterious Palette

ORIGINAL PALETTE—MYSTERIOUS

At first glance, it appears that the palette is limited to a variety of browns and black. A closer look reveals the important role of subtle bluish grays, purples, olives, rusts, and creams, without which the quilt would seem to flat. Note also how some blocks are composed of high-contrast strips while others are more muted. Varying the contrast from block to block contributes to the rich palette the artist successfully achieved.

Proportion

This palette is predominantly dark browns and blacks with a lesser amount of medium browns and a small measure of purples, ochres, blues, grays, burgundies, and creams.

Color Wheel

Although the palette is composed of predominantly analogous colors, some subtly complementary colors have been included in restrained amounts. Note also the broad use of the full range of values: lights, mediums, and darks. What cannot be captured in the color wheel is the complexity of the multi-colored prints used in the quilt. Using multicolored prints such as an orange overprint on a brown fabric lets the artist introduce small amounts of many hues without them dominating the quilt.

Analysis

Balance in color and value is often misunderstood by quilters to mean that there should be equal amounts of each color or value. This quilt allows one value and hue to dominate and uses other values and hues in perceptibly smaller amounts to provide depth and highlights to the palette. When a palette is predominantly dark, even the smallest amount of creams or yellows will stand out. Using prints that include small amounts of white or cream can be one way to bridge a value gap. For more inspiration on innovative uses of black, find images of Amish quilts. The Amish also know how to use black as a "bright."

Palette Variations

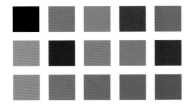

ORIGINAL PALETTE
MYSTERIOUS

These palette variations show how adding blues and greens from the other side of the color wheel to a predominantly brown-orange-ochre palette creates an entirely different mood. They also show how much stronger colors "read" when they are used in larger, contiguous arrangements rather than small, isolated pieces.

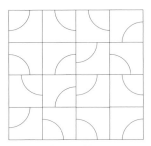

Drunkard's Path block

Variation 1
The introduction of just one blue transforms this palette from one that is "earthy" to one that is evocative of a moonlit evening.

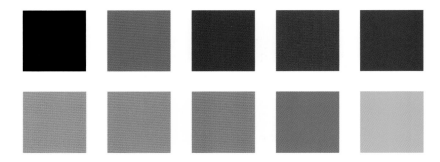

Variation 2
Adding one bright to an otherwise subtle palette makes the bright seem even brighter.

Variation 3
Medium-value colors appear lighter when surrounded by only darks.

Applying the Palettes to the Drunkard's Path Block

VARIATIONS IN HUE

ORIGINAL PALETTE—MYSTERIOUS

Variation 1

Variation 2

Variation 3

mysterious

Applying the Palettes to the Drunkard's Path Block

VARIATIONS IN VALUE

VARIATIONS IN PROPORTION

Color Workshop:
Black Is a Bright

While some quilters are comfortable with black, few look to it to create brilliance. Instead, most would opt for brilliant shades of red, hot pink, or purple. Black is too often considered funereal or dreary. Used in the right amount to provide contrast and with the right combination of hues, it is a bright. (See *Jewel Box* on page 118 of the Gallery).

INDIVIDUAL EXPLORATION

With your stash in front of you, close your eyes and pull out a fabric at random. Place it next to a piece of black fabric, either print or solid. Think about the colors you might add to these two fabrics that would make each appear more harmonious to the other. Keep adding fabrics until you feel that you have a harmonious palette. As you choose fabrics think about the general proportions of the colors. Is the black a sliver in a block, the perfect binding or the dominant hue in the palette?

GROUP EXPLORATION

This exploration is a sort of round robin that is designed to help each participant try new color combinations. Gather the members in a large circle with their stashes in front of them. Have the leader start the game with a black piece of fabric placed in the center of the circle. Starting with the person to the right of the leader, have each member of the circle add a fabric that complements the colors already introduced by the other members. Try to avoid ending up with twelve shades of one hue. The point is to see how black can mediate between both busy prints and muted ones. Discuss among the participants what worked and what didn't and why. Chances are your round robin palette will lead you in directions you would never have gone alone.

BEYOND THE QUILT

Place a piece of black paper on a table. One at a time, place various objects on top of it. Try things such as jewelry, fruit, leaves, a child's toy. In some instances, pile up a number of things on the paper so the black is barely visible. Look at the relationship between black and the other colors. Does the black appear depressing or does it make the other colors seem more vibrant? Notice how it makes the edges of light objects appear more crisp.

FESTIVE

Warm Greetings: Summer is anything but subtle. The hot palette of bright pinks, vibrant oranges, and bold magentas complement the sharp angles of the traditional Broken Dishes pattern. The small scale of the triangles also increases the visual complexity of the quilt. The varying sizes of spirals used in the quilting pattern add yet another layer of visual interest to the quilt.

WARM GREETINGS: SUMMER

36" × 36" (91 cm × 91 cm)
Weeks Ringle and Bill Kerr
of FunQuilts
2000

Cotton fabric and batting
Machine pieced and
machine quilted

Artists' Statement: "The inspiration for *Warm Greetings* was a flower bed planted with hundreds of zinnias. The zinnias could be categorized into hues of red, orange, and yellow with a great range of saturation and values that produced a vibrant display. The design and palette were chosen to convey the excitement a gardener feels at seeing such a profusion of color, found only a few months a year, after a winter of grays."

Festive Palette

ORIGINAL PALETTE—FESTIVE

The palette used in this quilt illustrates how the addition of one unexpected color and value can create surprising depth in a quilt. The pinks in the quilt range in value from pale pink to hot pink. The magentas come alive adjacent to the oranges. The surprise here is the rust-colored dark orange. This color adds considerable depth to the quilt that relies mostly on brighter colors of medium and light values.

Proportion

Lights and mediums are used in roughly equal proportions, while the darks are used sparingly. As darks can make a quilt seem visually heavy, using them in small amounts keeps the palette lively and bright.

Color Wheel

The analogous hues with high contrast created by light, medium, and dark values combined with the deep saturation of the oranges and pinks makes for a lively palette.

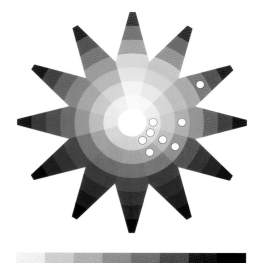

Analysis

There are three layers of color work and design in *Warm Greetings: Summer* that reinforce the big idea of the profusion of color found in a large massing of zinnias. The first is the palette abstracted from zinnias that often have small amounts of yellow in the center and green leaves and stems. But in a large mass planted outdoors, the green of the leaves and stems blends in to surrounding shrubs or grass, and the yellow disappears. The bold pinks, oranges, and magentas make a massing of these flowers powerful.

The second design element is the use of the Broken Dishes pattern, which complements the boldness of the colors with the strong, angular form of the triangles. Lastly, the dense, swirling pattern of the stitching using bold orange thread adds an additional contrast element—making the quilt as lively and festive as a bouquet of zinnias.

Palette Variations

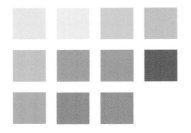

ORIGINAL PALETTE
FESTIVE

These palettes demonstrate that highly saturated colors, even when paired with desaturated, softer tones, will still be perceived as bold. Introducing complementary hues or eliminating less saturated colors makes the palette even louder.

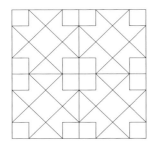

Sawtooth Star block

Variation 1
Excluding the lightest values and introducing more yellows and oranges into the festive palette creates a louder palette.

Variation 2
Judicious use of blue, violet, and green, mixed with the most saturated colors of the original palette, creates an equally lively palette.

Variation 3
As these colors are so vibrant together, a festive palette can be created from as few as four colors.

Applying the Palettes to the Sawtooth Star Block

VARIATIONS IN HUE

ORIGINAL PALETTE—FESTIVE

Variation 1

Variation 2

Variation 3

festive

Applying the Palettes to the Sawtooth Star Block

VARIATIONS IN VALUE

VARIATIONS IN PROPORTION

Color Workshop:
Color, Personality, and Proportion

Quilts can be about many things: a traditional block, a narrative, a color palette. The challenge met in *Warm Greetings: Summer* was to develop a palette that evoked a bed of zinnias. In the same way that a palette can remind you of a certain flower, it can also be used to express the personality of an individual.

Start thinking about color in relation to people you know. When you think of your friend Mary, cool blue may come to mind because she is quiet and reserved, with a gentle disposition. Your cousin Bob may remind you of olives and browns because of his dark complexion and hazel eyes. Thoughts of your mother may recall primary colors because you think of her as straightforward and strong. Understanding the personalities of colors will help you make appropriate color choices in your quilts.

INDIVIDUAL EXPLORATION

Create a family portrait in fabric. Represent each member of your family as a 3" × 3" (8 cm × 8 cm) block made of thin strips of fabric. You don't need to sew these, just cut strips and use a glue stick to put them on cardboard or stiff paper. Consider the colors and amounts of each color you use. Show them to your family and see their reactions.

GROUP EXPLORATION

Divide yourselves into smaller groups of no more than four people each. Each member should represent themselves and the other members of the group as a 3" × 3" (8 cm × 8 cm) square made of thin strips of fabric. You don't need to sew these, just cut strips and use a glue stick to put each one on a separate piece of cardboard or stiff paper, but be sure to label each with the person's name. Consider the colors and amounts of each color you use.

When finished, group the portraits so you can see the many ways of representing each individual. Take turns explaining how you chose the fabrics and proportions. Part of developing color confidence is learning to talk about your design and color decisions.

BEYOND THE QUILT

Stop by your local library and check out a few books on fashion through the ages—don't just limit yourself to current fashions, but think about color palettes that were in vogue decades ago. Think of the popularity of pastels in the 40s and 50s or the psychedelic colors of the 60s and 70s. Another source for inspiration is a natural history museum that will have depictions of people from around the world in their native garb. Whether it is the brilliant feather capes of ancient Hawaii or the luxurious silk gowns of Korea, you will find timeless color combinations.

festive

LUMINOUS

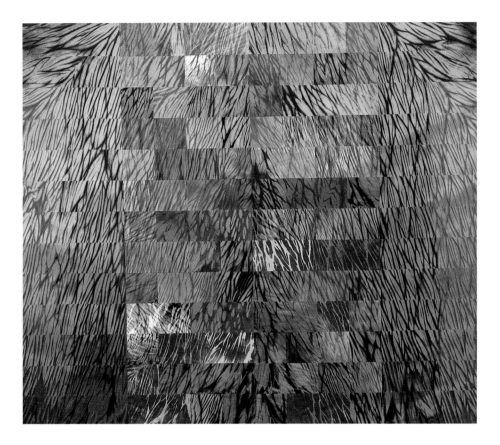

Although there are more colors in this quilt than can be easily placed on a color wheel, the quilt is unified by a simple composition of horizontal strips that use symmetry as their organizing element. The contrast between the irregular diagonal lines of the shibori dyeing technique and the orthogonal lines of the piecing create yet another layer of visual complexity. The luminosity of this quilt is created by the subtle value differences in each of the shibori pieces.

AGAPE

60" × 52" (152 cm × 132 cm)
Jan Myers-Newbury
1997
Cotton fabric, polyester batting
Cotton muslin, dyed with Procion MX dyes in arashi shibori techniques
Machine pieced and machine quilted
Hand-signed in embroidery

Artist's Statement: "*Agape* is one of those quilts that began with leftovers. The central section employs some fairly small pieces of fabric chosen not only for color but for the directional flow of the linear patterning. The compression in the center became a pivotal motif in the quilt. The two side panels were specifically dyed for the work. *Agape* is a Greek word for love (somewhat in opposition—or complementary to—Eros), referring to the love that extends outward and is freely given; the grace of God."

Luminous Palette

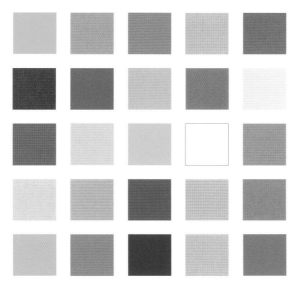

ORIGINAL PALETTE—LUMINOUS

This palette, when seen as swatches, immediately reveals the broad range of color that is subtly distributed in the quilt. Greens, violets, blues, reds, and oranges appear in values ranging from light to dark, a product of the dying process. The contrast between the light and dark values creates the luminosity.

Proportion

Proportion is the key to the success of *Agape*. Many of the medium greens and grays of the quilt appear even darker than they are because they contrast with the more-abundant lighter values. The side panels of yellow-greens provide a surface against which small amounts of blue and red-orange have a chance to shine.

Color Wheel

There is a nearly infinite range of color in these lush, hand-dyed fabrics that cannot be fully represented on the color wheel, rather the purpose of mapping out the palette on the color wheel is to show the wide distribution of both hues and values.

Analysis

Hand-dyed fabrics can easily overpower a quilt when used indiscriminately. But when used masterfully, as they are here, they create a dramatic work united by a richness of color and light. The yellow-green side panels of this quilt are linked to the richly colored center with the fluid lines of the shibori dying, carefully placed on a diagonal. Careful attention is placed to the proportion and placement of color, most noticeably in the single square of blue, just off center. This quilt serves as a reminder that luminosity elevates even the most sophisticated color work to another level.

Palette Variations

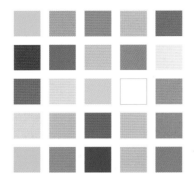

ORIGINAL PALETTE
LUMINOUS

The overall mood of the quilt is not just determined by the colors in the palette but in how the colors are organized. These quilts are all based on the Wild Goose Chase block but vary in spirit a great deal. Using color in bands or in a regulated order can create more calm than using the same colors in a random arrangement.

Variation 1
While there is still luminosity in this palette, eliminating the reds and oranges reduces the sparkle.

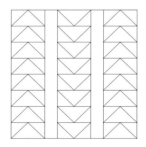

Wild Goose Chase block

Variation 2
Without darks or lights, this palette becomes even more quiet.

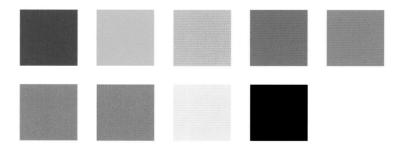

Variation 3
Introducing black and white transforms the quilt into a more graphic composition.

Applying the Palettes to the Wild Goose Chase Block

VARIATIONS IN HUE

ORIGINAL PALETTE—LUMINOUS

Variation 1

Variation 2

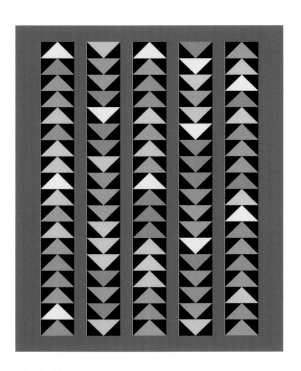

Variation 3

Applying the Palettes to the Wild Goose Chase Block

VARIATIONS IN VALUE

VARIATIONS IN PROPORTION

Color Workshop:
Complements

When looking at the color wheel, most people easily understand the concept of complementary colors. But how about determining the complements of more subtle hues? These explorations will help you fine-tune your eye to see the subtle hues in everyday objects.

INDIVIDUAL EXPLORATION

Gather ten objects with desaturated coloration. Some can be from a park or garden, others can be from your pantry, still others might be from your laundry basket. With a color wheel or your stash in front of you, try to determine which hue is the complement to the color of the object you've chosen. Here are some items you might want to include in your exploration: an eggplant, cinnamon, turmeric, dried basil, a pinecone, any sort of dried bean, sand, a glass of apple juice, leaves, a red potato, celery, any sort of cheese, any variety of pears. These subtle complements are often used in quilts with beautiful color work, but we don't realize that they are complementary colors because we are so accustomed to thinking of complementary colors as the bright, saturated colors on a color wheel.

BEYOND THE QUILT

Visit a florist, keeping in mind the role of complements when arranging flowers. As the stems of most flowers are green, any red in a flower will appear vibrant. Is this the reason, perhaps, that red roses are so popular? While you're there, buy a flower with especially beautiful coloring. Throughout the following week, try to think about the color of the flower. Is it the same all over? Is the throat of the flower the same as the edges? Look at the back of the flower and where the flower meets the stem. Think about the complements to each of these subtle shades.

GROUP EXPLORATION

Ask each member of the group to bring a few small squares of fabric of muted or desaturated color. Try as a group to develop a color wheel using these muted colors. Include, if possible, value differences as well. Design a challenge for each member to create a block using these colors. Assemble all of the blocks and use the quilt as a fund-raiser.

luminous

GRAPHIC

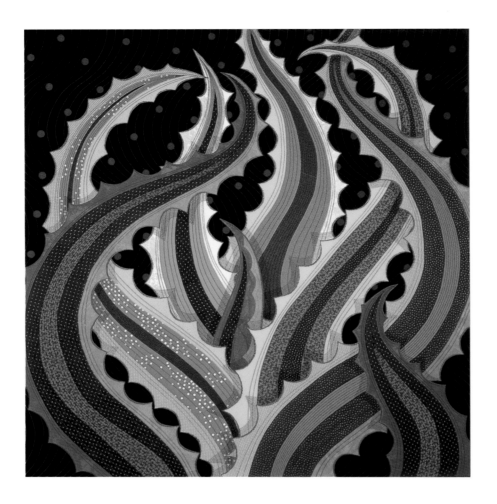

Comedians agree that the key to a good impersonation is finding a quirk in a person's mannerisms and exaggerating it greatly. Similarly, Jane Sassaman manages to capture the quality of plants through her quilts. The exaggerated forms represent more than the physical characteristics of each plant—they represent the wild, untamed growth of the whole plant world. The elegant curves and intertwined tips in *Century Plant* contrast with the prickly edges of the leaves, capturing the exuberant growth of this exotic species. This plant appears so wild that it might outgrow the quilt at any moment. Monochromatic prints in complementary colors against a black backdrop reinforce the larger-than-life form of the plant.

CENTURY PLANT

54" × 52" (137 cm × 132 cm)
Jane A. Sassaman
2000

Cotton fabric, cotton batting
Machine appliquéd,
machine quilted

Artist's Statement: "This idealized century plant combines the exotic characteristics of many desert plants. In real life, this plant is dramatic because of its scale and shape, not for its color—a dull gray-green. Sunlight interacts with the three-dimensional leaves creating shadows and severe definitions.

But a quilt is only two-dimensional, so we must rely on color to create the illusion of light and depth. By making a majority of the leaves in stripes that radiate from dark in the center to light on the edges, the gentle, concave curve of each leaf is implied. Also, the outside of each leaf is a 'sunshine color' instead of realistic green. These colors graduate from light yellow in the center to rust in the outside leaves. This makes the plant look like it's radiating from within."

Graphic Palette

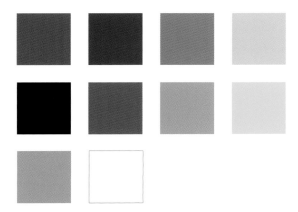

ORIGINAL PALETTE—GRAPHIC

This palette is spare, using colors that offer contrast in both value and hue. Note how the edges of the leaves are the strongest point of contrast in the entire quilt, emphasizing both the intense color and form of the edges. Imagine how different this quilt would be without the color and the prickliness of those edges. Imagine also how less dramatic the quilt would be without the black background.

Color Wheel

Part of what is so wonderful about this quilt is the lively use of the bright reds and oranges as complements to the greens and the whites as complements to the black. Note how the colors on the color wheel are not clustered as analogous colors would be but, rather, are spread around the color wheel both in terms of hue and value.

Proportion

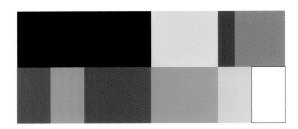

Although nearly a quarter of this quilt is black, the yellows, greens, and reds are what jump out because of their high contrast and saturation. The strong, prickly form of the reds, oranges, yellows, and whites are so dynamic that they appear to be a larger portion of the quilt than they actually are.

Analysis

Century Plant shows quilters the power of starting with a big idea. In this case, it was to capture the essence of an idealized plant. The colors, form, composition, and fabric selection work together to express the form and character of the plant. While color is an important part of this quilt, the big idea is about more than just color and succeeds at all levels.

Palette Variations

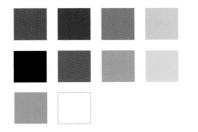

ORIGINAL PALETTE
GRAPHIC

The graphic palette offers strong contrasts, used to reinforce edges and the sharpness of the forms. The inclusion of black makes the contrast between other hues in the palette that much sharper. The traditional Log Cabin block combined with a graphic palette yields clearly defined patterns.

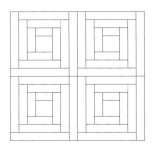

Log Cabin block

Variation 1
Removing all light values flattens the palette, making the quilt more subdued.

Variation 2
These saturated, slightly dark primaries and secondaries along with black make the yellows and oranges "pop."

Variation 3
Including more light values and placing them adjacent to black in the quilt is highly graphic.

Applying the Palettes to the Log Cabin Block

VARIATIONS IN HUE

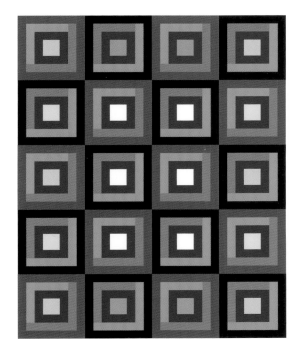

ORIGINAL PALETTE—GRAPHIC

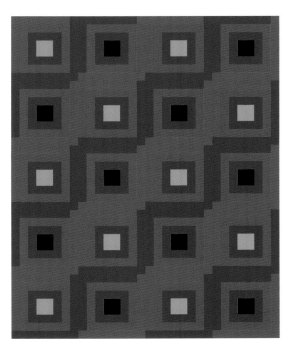

Variation 1

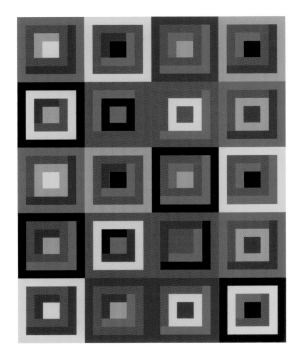

Variation 2

Variation 3

graphic

Applying the Palettes to the Log Cabin Block

VARIATIONS IN VALUE

VARIATIONS IN PROPORTION

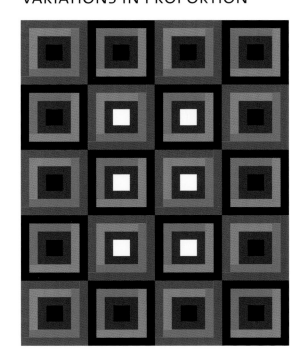 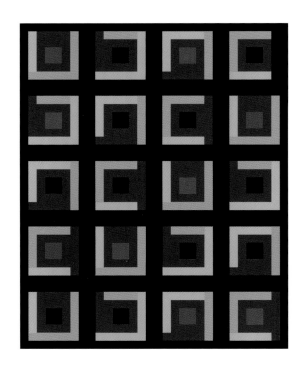

Color Workshop:
Color and the Senses

Just as Jane Sassaman developed a palette that expresses the character of a century plant, including its prickliness, you can also think about how a palette of colors can express a sensory experience. How would you develop a "smooth" palette versus a "rough" palette? What would a "sharp" palette look like? A "rubbery" palette?

INDIVIDUAL EXPLORATION

Choose an object in your home that is either sharp, rough, smooth, cold, hot, or has some other property that evokes a sensation when touched. Try putting together a palette of colors that would be expressive of that sensation. For example, a rough object might have a lot of contrast while a smooth one would have very little. How might the palette change if it were, for example, both cold and rough? Or smooth and hot?

GROUP EXPLORATION

Have the leader place in a bag objects that have textures or other sensorial characteristics such as an emery board, a bumpy gourd, a stuffed animal, a smooth stone, a gumball from a Sweetgum tree, a scouring pad, etc. Have the members of the group place their hands in the bag without looking. Each participant should think about the first object touched and develop a palette of colors from their stashes that is expressive of the object. Have participants discuss how they made decisions about which color evoked which sensation.

BEYOND THE QUILT

Read the Sunday comics from your local newspaper to see how cartoonists have developed palettes that convey the tone of their comic strips. *Peanuts* cartoons that are light in tone are generally illustrated with clear tints of primary colors. *Boondocks*, for example, which often deals with issues of politics and race, has a very subdued, serious palette of browns and oranges. Think about how different the perception of the comic strip would be if the palettes of these two comics were switched.

INTENSE

DIVORCE QUILT

95" × 75" (241 cm × 191 cm)
Katharine Brainard
1990

*Cotton fabrics, cotton/poly blends,
cotton batting, embroidery floss,
beads, buttons, sequins, etc.*

*Machine and hand pieced, machine
appliquéd and hand appliquéd,
machine quilted, hand embroidered,
and hand embellished*

Images can stay with you a long time. This 1990 quilt is so powerful, people are still talking about it. The forms and narrative are emotionally intense, and the color work is unforgettable. Deeply saturated red with highlights of bright yellow, deep purple, and neon green contrast with the stark black and white. This color work supports the design intention: an angry quilt with screaming colors.

Artist's Statement: "The *Divorce Quilt* colors convey emotion. Red signifies anger and passion; blacks and blues (like a bruise on the heart) signify the pain of a difficult passage in life. Small areas of bright yellow and neon green, strategically placed to balance one another out, provide zing. Scattered white pearls (a broken necklace) and ivory satin buttons (reminiscent of a wedding gown) join crystal teardrop shapes (tears) raining down the sashing. The sashing and borders are the only square elements. The blocks are all slightly off kilter, cut at angles rather than square—because sometimes things in life just don't square up."

Intense Palette

ORIGINAL PALETTE—INTENSE

This palette is all about saturation and contrast. There is no attempt to soften the edges here. Nor should there be. Doing so would undermine the big idea. Bright, bold, colors, stark white, and deep black. Simple. Powerful.

Proportion

Red, black, and white are used in similar amounts but in different ways. The red sashing appears dominant because it is used in long, contiguous pieces. The black and white are used more sporadically, often in black-and-white printed fabrics that serve as a backdrop for text or images. Yellows, greens, purples, and flesh tones are used in small amounts.

Color Wheel

No analogous colors, no subtle value shifts are used. A more complex palette would have detracted from the intensity of the piece. Note how each of the colors used is the most saturated version of that hue on the color wheel. There are a few highlights of flesh tones used for the feet and the Cat Woman mask, but the palette is mostly restricted to red, white, black, purple, yellow, and green.

Analysis

Not everyone feels comfortable depicting intense emotion in their quilts, but this quilt shows that when you begin with a focused idea, the color work often comes more naturally than when you just happen on a pleasing fabric in a fabric store. The idea gives you a strong direction. Sometimes just having to talk through an idea, explaining what you're trying to convey, will help give you direction and help you with your color choices.

Palette Variations

ORIGINAL PALETTE
INTENSE

There is no ambiguity in these palettes. These saturated colors are in sharp contrast with each other, and there is no pattern that would render these colors gentle. Note the variations that contain black and white. A proliferation of other hues can mediate the sharp contrast between black and white, but when there are few colors available to mediate them, the palette becomes more stark.

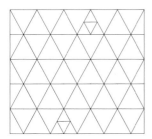

Thousand Pyramids pattern

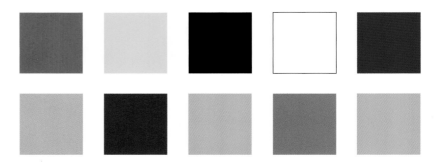

Variation 1
Adding a warm orange and rich purple to the palette adds warmth and depth.

Variation 2
A small palette of only saturated colors can become flat when there is minimal value contrast.

Variation 3
Black and white become quite stark when there are few colors to bridge the contrast between them.

Applying the Palettes to the Thousand Pyramids Pattern

VARIATIONS IN HUE

ORIGINAL PALETTE—INTENSE

Variation 1

Variation 2

Variation 3

Applying the Palettes to the Thousand Pyramids Pattern

VARIATIONS IN VALUE

VARIATIONS IN PROPORTION

Color Workshop:
Color and Emotion

Photographers often say, "Shoot what you know. The more you know about something, the better you can portray it." The same can be said about making a narrative quilt. Each person has events in their lives of intense emotional power—happy, sad, fearful, regrettable. These events are often treasure troves of big ideas.

INDIVIDUAL EXPLORATION

Find a quiet place where you can be alone without distraction. Think about the most powerful moment in your life—happy or sad. How would you express it in colors? Think especially about whites and blacks, lights and darks. If you feel comfortable doing so, sketch a palette or design with colored pencils.

GROUP EXPLORATION

In every group of people, there is someone who is experiencing some wonderful life event or some tragic one. As a group, design a small "healing" block for someone experiencing a difficult life event or a "celebration" block for someone in the midst of a happy event. Discuss which colors would be appropriate. Are they muted or bold? Is it narrative or abstract? Think about the associations of color that this person might have in their life. A favorite sweater, the color of their house, a favorite food. Regardless of the quality of the color work, it is certain to become a treasured gift to its recipient.

BEYOND THE QUILT

On the Internet or at your local library, find images of war rugs from Afghanistan from the 1980s when Afghanistan was at war with the former Soviet Union. These rugs bring together the rich Afghani textile tradition with the contemporary issues of its society. Look at the way in which rug designers portrayed the war through both color and form.

ETHEREAL

The soft, muted colors used in this quilt create a dreamy, ethereal quality. With the exception of the black used in the star, the rest of the quilt is composed of soft edges and minimal value and hue contrasts. This quilt proves that black can be incorporated in a palette and still retain the gentle feel of the design. In the center of the star, the intense pinks and greens are used in a way reminiscent of the intense color found in the center of an iris.

**KALEIDOSCOPIC XXI:
THE THANK YOUR LUCKY
STAR MEMORIAL QUILT**

45" × 46" (114 cm × 117 cm)
Paula Nadelstern
2000

*Cottons and silk fabrics
with polyester batting*
*Machine pieced and
hand quilted*

Artist's Statement: "To its maker, every quilt becomes a soft document, chronicling the events that took place during its evolution. In this case, what began as a requiem for one family member turned into a celebration of another loved one's survival."

Ethereal Palette

ORIGINAL PALETTE—ETHEREAL

Creams and pastels dominate the quilt with the only saturation appearing at the center of the star. Other than the leap in contrast between the creams, medium pinks, blues, and the black in the star, the rest of the palette consists of subtleties in hue and value that make each color appear to bleed into the next with a kind of muted iridescence.

Proportion

Desaturated colors in medium values dominate the palette with small amounts of more saturated pinks, greens, and blues used as highlights. Although the black appears dominant in the quilt because of its contrast with the other fabrics and its central location within the composition, it makes up only about one eighth of the quilt.

Color Wheel

The dreamy, watercolorlike quality of the borders of the quilt as well as the small stars is created from fabrics with minimal contrast in value. This is particularly evident on the color wheel where the dots are clustered in just a few values and in analogous colors.

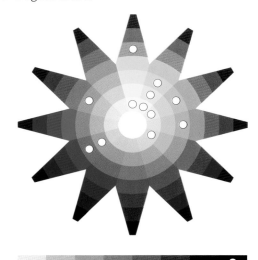

Analysis

Although the kaleidoscopic forms in Paula Nadelstern's quilts are generally graphic with clear forms and crisp edges, the field on which they are set are often soft or even blurry. In this quilt, she carries out that contrast fully—she has been very intentional in her selection of hues, values, and levels of saturation. Allowing some edges to be blurry and others to be clean results not only in interesting color juxtapositions but also in the ethereal quality appropriate for a memorial quilt.

Palette Variations

Varying saturation within the palette softens or intensifies the mood of the quilt. The pointed form of the triangle used in Wild Goose Chase exaggerates the contrast in value and hue. These variations also demonstrate how including black in a palette changes the overall balance of color.

ORIGINAL PALETTE
ETHEREAL

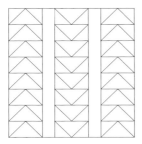

Wild Goose Chase block

Variation 1
Removing the black and simplifying the spectrum of hues mutes the entire palette.

Variation 2
Pairing muted earth tones with pastels yields a gentle palette.

Variation 3
Reducing the original palette to its most saturated components by eliminating the pastels makes the palette more graphic and slightly less ethereal.

Applying the Palettes to the Wild Goose Chase Block

VARIATIONS IN HUE

ORIGINAL PALETTE—ETHEREAL

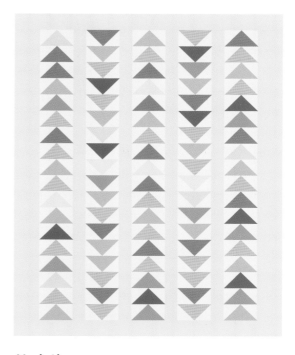

Variation 1

Variation 2

Variation 3

Applying the Palettes to the Wild Goose Chase Block

VARIATIONS IN VALUE

VARIATIONS IN PROPORTION

Color Workshop:
Color Blending

In recent years, many quilters have experimented with "watercolor" quilts, which generally feature a value fade from light to dark. Using the principles of watercolor quilts, take the opportunity to experiment with fading not just from one value to another but from one hue to another. Consulting a watercolor quilt book from the library or your local bookstore or quilt shop will be helpful if you've never made a watercolor quilt.

INDIVIDUAL EXPLORATION

What is the dominant color in your stash? What's second? Try to make a 12" (30 cm) finished block out of 1" (3 cm) finished squares that fade from one color to another. For example, if you want to fade from blue to red, you would start with blues, transition to purple, and then end with red. If you need to, consult the color wheel for which hues might help you transition between the colors you've chosen.

GROUP EXPLORATION

This exploration works best with a large group. Tell all of the participants ahead of time to wear a solid colored top (not white or black) of any color for the gathering. Once everyone has arrived, create a human color wheel by having the participants organize themselves along the color spectrum according to the color of their tops. If there are gaps in the color wheel, have the people next to the gap hold pieces of fabric to complete the spectrum. Pay attention to value differences as well. Appoint a caller, like at a square dance. That caller should randomly call out some of these orders for you to follow: rearrange yourselves by value from lightest to darkest, pair off in complementary colors, group into primaries and secondaries, pair off into analogous pairs, etc. In addition to having some fun, this exploration should help you fine tune your understanding of the color wheel.

BEYOND THE QUILT

Find a picture in a magazine that has a color fade of some sort. It might be a photograph of a sunset that fades from blue to orange or a beach shot in which the white of the sand fades to the deep blue of the ocean. Draw a grid on top of the image with the lines 1" (3 cm) apart (or smaller if need be). Cut up the picture along the lines until you have a pile of 1" (3 cm) squares. Now look at the individual squares and note the differences in the colors. Try to reassemble the picture using your understanding of value changes and hue fades.

ethereal

UNDERSTATED

Beautifully composed, this quilt allows the subtleties of the traditional Japanese indigos to glow by including minimal value contrasts elsewhere in the quilt. But perhaps the most delightful aspect of the colorwork here is found in the red ties used to finish the quilt. These ties are reminiscent of, yet different from, the Japanese embroidery tradition known as sashiko. They enliven an otherwise dark quilt, offering it both texture and another layer of color complexity.

OUT OF THE BLUE

20" × 33" (51 cm × 84 cm)
Angie Woolman
1997

*Predominant use of
antique and contemporary
Japanese fabrics
Machine pieced, overtied*

Artist's Statement: "This small piece was a study of the use of an accent color in the context of indigo-dyed Japanese yukata fabrics. The red accent was used with much attention to proportion of red (to dark blue) and its placement. More important than finding the right red fabric was the use of large-gesture fabrics that contained some red. Bright red ties were added as an answer to the need for just a bit more red."

Understated Palette

ORIGINAL PALETTE—UNDERSTATED

Deep indigo blues dominate this palette with red, light blue, and white highlights providing contrast in the center strip. This is a very restrained palette, appropriate to the traditional Japanese cloth used here. Had more white been included, the prints of the indigo fabrics would not have read as clearly. The addition of olive is an unexpected touch that enriches the quilt without competing with the other fabrics.

Proportion

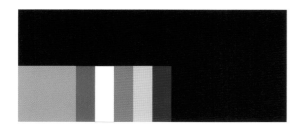

A good three-quarters of this quilt is dark blue, but the grid of small red ties breaks up the darkness of the blue making it seem less dominant. White, light blue, and red are shown in only small amounts, but their presence seems larger because they are in such strong contrast to the darkness of the indigo. The olive has much less contrast with the indigo and thus seems smaller than it is.

Color Wheel

This is a very simple palette: indigo blue, red, olive, and white. Two dominant hues used in different amounts allow the complexity of the large scale prints to be read without distraction. Think about how differently this quilt would look with oranges, yellows, or greens added to it. Some fabrics, such as these indigos, call for a simple palette.

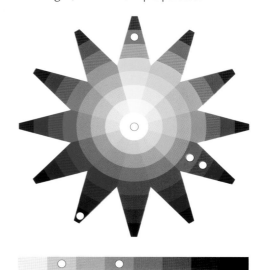

Analysis

Perhaps the most important color lesson to be learned from this quilt is in the use of the red ties. Quilters often put all of their energy into the colorwork and design of the quilt top—and the quilting and binding become an afterthought. Other quilters worry about the color of the quilting thread showing and quilt with monofilament so it doesn't show. In fact, many of the sample quilts that hang in quilt shops are neither quilted nor bound. They are simply pieced quilt tops created to show off a given pattern, palette, or fabric. This is a missed opportunity. *Out of the Blue* is an excellent example of how contrast in the quilting and binding of the quilt transforms the quilt top. This quilt encourages quilters to use contrasting thread or binding.

Palette Variations

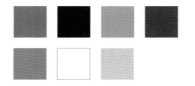

ORIGINAL PALETTE
UNDERSTATED

These palettes show how changes in the number of colors and in the proportions in which they are used greatly alter the mood of a quilt. By increasing or decreasing the amount of indigo blue in each of the palettes, the overall color balance changes markedly.

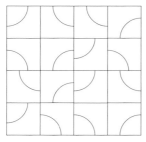

Drunkard's Path block

Variation 1
Without the dark blue, this palette becomes much softer as does the appearance of the Drunkard's Path block.

Variation 2
Replacing the soft gray and white with dark pinks and reds makes the palette much bolder.

Variation 3
Fewer colors make this palette appear more graphic.

Applying the Palettes to the Drunkard's Path Block

VARIATIONS IN HUE

ORIGINAL PALETTE—UNDERSTATED

Variation 1

Variation 2

Variation 3

Applying the Palettes to the Drunkard's Path Block

VARIATIONS IN VALUE

VARIATIONS IN PROPORTION

Color Workshop: Changing Light

The famous quote by Mies van der Rohe, the twentieth-century architect, "God is in the details" is a good reminder to all quilters. Many quilters do not consider the role of the quilting and binding at the beginning of the project, nor do they think about how the quilting and binding might be part of the big idea. Although there are quilts in which the quilting and binding should have a minimal role in the overall design, there are also many quilts that would be made more interesting by different quilting or a sophisticated binding. These explorations should give you a chance to try out a few approaches and see what you think.

INDIVIDUAL EXPLORATION

Color on a spool of thread is so different from the way the color appears as a single width of thread. When you start your next quilt, make a color sampler by gathering together some scraps of the fabrics you intend to use and sewing them into a block at least 12" × 12" (30 cm × 30 cm). Cut a piece of backing fabric and piece of the batting you intend to use and baste it together as you would any larger quilt. Before you even begin piecing the quilt top, try out some different colors of thread on the sampler. Don't look at the thread on the spool, rather, place one strand of thread across the main colors of the quilt and then stand back 8 to 10 feet (2.4 to 3 m) and look at it again. Don't limit yourself to the hues that are in the quilt. Try others hues, other values. Try a bright yellow or a soft gray, even red. What would a contrasting thread or binding add to your next quilt?

GROUP EXPLORATION

Have each participant baste together a color sampler as described previously. Place all of the samplers in a large bag. Have each person reach into the bag and grab a block on which to experiment. Each person will experiment with different quilting threads or bindings. When everyone is done, have the designer of the original sampler and the person who experimented with the threads and binding talk about each of their approaches to the palette. While you may not want to adopt the suggestions of the other person into your final quilt, this is a wonderful opportunity to get a fresh interpretation from someone with a different aesthetic.

BEYOND THE QUILT

Whenever you are in a tiled room, notice the grout color. Although many bathrooms are grouted with white grout, sometimes the grout is tinted. Grout used in floors is often tinted. Sometimes it is tinted the same color of the tile, sometimes it is tinted to a beige or gray. Think about whether the role of the grout is to differentiate each tile or to make the whole surface appear unified.

understated

MELLOW

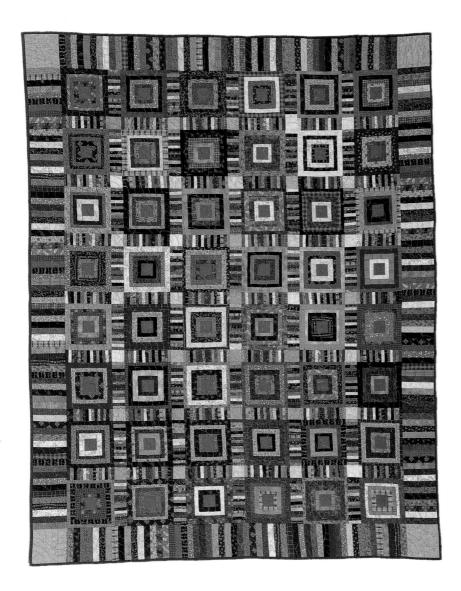

The difference between a good watercolor painting and a great one is often in how the artist uses the white (or non-painted areas) of the paper in relation to the painted areas. If the artist paints every inch of the paper, they are said to have "killed" their whites. The more astute artist uses the white of paper as the most powerful color in the palette. While the rich burgundy tint throughout this quilt lends it the "mellowness" its designer intended, the bright creams, pale yellows, and mustards play the same role as the white of the paper, adding a sparkle and bringing the quilt to life. Were it not for the occasional lights in this quilt, it would look as if someone had dipped the entire quilt in wine, deadening the color.

CABIN TRACKS

66" × 85" (168 cm × 216 cm)
Judy Hasheider,
machine quilted
by Linda Diny
2001

Cotton fabric and cotton/ polyester batting

Machine pieced and machine quilted

Artist's Statement: "This quilt was inspired by an antique quilt. I did my own take on the design. The colors used were not planned or thought through, but just evolved because they felt right. I like combining different prints, and each one seems to tell me where to go next. I was trying to achieve an old, antique look with a mellowness but, yet, give it a twist of bright. Thus the mustard color seemed to speak to me."

Mellow Palette

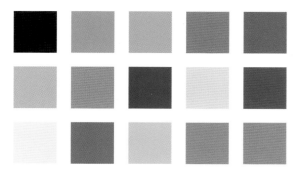

ORIGINAL PALETTE—MELLOW

This palette is primarily composed of burgundy hues with undertones of brown, purple, beige, and red. Pale yellows, creams, and mustards are subtle complements to the purples elsewhere in the quilt. There are also small amounts of black, which provide value contrast.

Proportion

About 70 percent of this quilt is burgundy or its color wheel neighbors purple and red. The balance of the palette is split between creams, yellows, mustards, and black.

Color Wheel

There is not enough room on the color wheel to capture all of the subtle shades of burgundy included in this quilt. Although the creams, yellows, and mustards appear separately on the color wheel, each of the fabrics used in this hue features a red or burgundy overprint that prevents introducing too sharp of a contrast to an otherwise mellow palette.

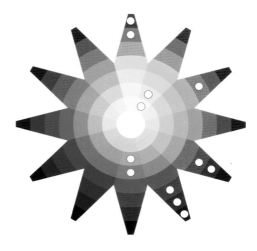

Analysis

Although the temptation among quilters is often to buy and cut equal amounts of every color to be included in the quilt, this is an excellent example of how using more of one hue or value than another produces a more interesting quilt. Using light values sparingly as highlights in an otherwise dark quilt often produces a glowing, rich effect. Darker values used in an otherwise lighter-value quilt often appear as shadows.

mellow

Palette Variations

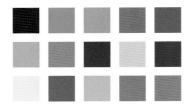

**ORIGINAL PALETTE
MELLOW**

These palettes and quilt variations are good studies in proportion. When each color is used in equal proportions, the palette seems much brighter. In the original quilt the composition was dominated by dark green. Substituting other hues or using the original hue in smaller amounts results in a much brighter palette.

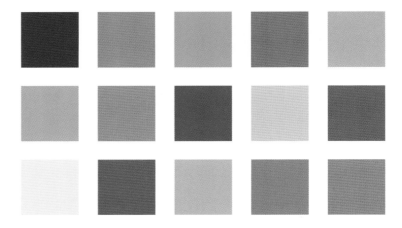

Variation 1

Introducing several shades of blue totally transforms this palette into a more lively mix of colors.

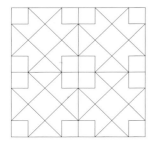

Sawtooth Star block

Variation 2

Eliminating the lightest values creates a rich, yet flatter, composition.

Variation 3

More value contrasts with fewer hues make the palette appear bolder.

Applying the Palettes to the Sawtooth Star Block

VARIATIONS IN HUE

ORIGINAL PALETTE—MELLOW

Variation 1

Variation 2

Variation 3

Applying the Palettes to the Sawtooth Star Block

VARIATIONS IN VALUE

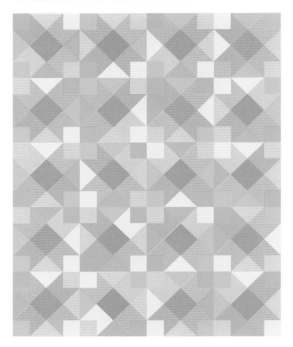

VARIATIONS IN PROPORTION

Color Workshop:
Color in Depth

Cabin Tracks shows the importance of hue contrast. Although the burgundy tint of the quilt is pleasing, it would become flat without the hue and value contrast provided by the creams, yellows, and mustards. The following explorations are designed to help you determine when a palette based on one hue can unite a quilt and when it overwhelms it.

INDIVIDUAL EXPLORATION

Gather some small scraps of fabric from your stash that you don't plan to use. Place them in a saucepan with four or five tea bags depending on how many scraps you have. Fill the pan with enough boiling water to cover the fabric. Allow the tea to sit until the fabrics have been noticeably stained by the tea. Drain the pan and squeeze out the excess tea from the fabric. Allow the fabric to dry on a trash bag so the tea doesn't stain your work area. Once dry, gather the scraps together. They will appear similar now that they have all been dyed with the same tint. Are they a pleasing palette? Add a few scraps of fabric that were not dyed with the tea bags. Do they enliven the palette or appear too bright? This exercise should help you determine when using one color can be a good thing—and when it can be too much of a good thing.

GROUP EXPLORATION

Have everyone in your group bring in ten 3" (8 cm) squares of fabric. Sort the fabrics on a table according to the twelve segments of the color wheel. Have each person take the fabrics from one segment of the color wheel. (If you have more than twelve people in your group, you will need to make multiple color wheels or subdivide the segments.) Look carefully at these fabrics, then create a palette that includes other hues from your stash. If, for example, you selected the red pile, was it originally harmonious? How did the palette change by adding say a yellow or green to the reds?

BEYOND THE QUILT

Invest a couple of dollars in an inexpensive watercolor set. While these sets are not appropriate for serious painting, they are excellent for learning how to mix colors. Develop several palettes by dabbing different colors of paint onto the back of index cards. Be sure to clean your brush in clear water periodically to make sure the colors don't get too muddy. Take these palettes to the fabric store with you next time you go to buy fabric.

mellow

GALLERY

NEW DIRECTIONS

74" × 92" (188 cm × 234 cm)
Bill Kerr and Weeks Ringle
of FunQuilts
2002

Cotton fabric and batting
Machine pieced and
machine quilted

Artists' Statement: "This quilt has the softness of a well-worn pair of jeans. Many of our quilts are made from saturated jewel tones or mono-chromatic prints. *New Directions* is an attempt to bring together a softer, gentle palette of multicolored prints with minimal value contrast. While some of our quilts explore the value differences in one hue, this quilt does the opposite. Our challenge was to see how many hues we could add to provide richness while limiting the value range to prevent the colorwork from becoming busy. The staggered cream triangles create unity among the diverse fabrics and add visual depth."

GROUND COVER I

28" × 57" (71 cm × 145 cm)
Jane A. Sassaman
2001

Cotton fabric and batting
Machine appliquéd and
machine quilted

Artist's Statement: "A garden gets its character from the interaction between contrasting groups of shapes, colors, and textures. A forest floor is the same. There is organization because plants grow in clumps. But there is randomness, too. Think of bluebells in the spring growing with ferns and grasses. The forest floor in *Ground Cover I* is composed of three groups: the large leaves, the leaves on white stems with a blue flower, and the yellow flower with green leaves. Each group has its own palette. Just like nature, there is green everywhere, but many different greens. The white stems and flower add a sparkle that helps to tie all the groups together, too. All these elements are appliquéd to a black background that makes all the hand-dyed colors even richer."

OF CURRENT AND TIDE

63" × 75" (160 cm × 191 cm)
Heather Waldron Tewell
2000

*Cotton fabric and batting,
acrylic yarn*

*Machine pieced and
machine quilted*

Artist's Statement: "Because my work begins with nature, my color choices start with what I see. In summer, the bay out my living room window is vivid blue, the sand bar is taupe, and the rocky shore is gray. But they never stay the same for long. Five different shades in each horizontal area reflect these changes of color over time. Applying the theory of the Pointillists, I used many colors of thread in the quilting believing that the viewers' eyes would blend them to approximate the complexity of colors from the sky reflected in the water."

LAKE SUPERIOR GOLD

58" × 73" (147 cm × 185 cm)
Gloria Spaete
2002

*Cotton fabric, 80/20 cotton/
polyester batting*

*Machine pieced and
machine quilted*

Artist's Statement: "In October, my husband and I were vacationing in Canada. The fall colors peeked on the day we drove home. From Canada to southern Wisconsin, their brilliance was breathtaking. It was a continuous, spectacular array of color. I wanted to capture those colors in a quilt, so when I got home, I made this quilt."

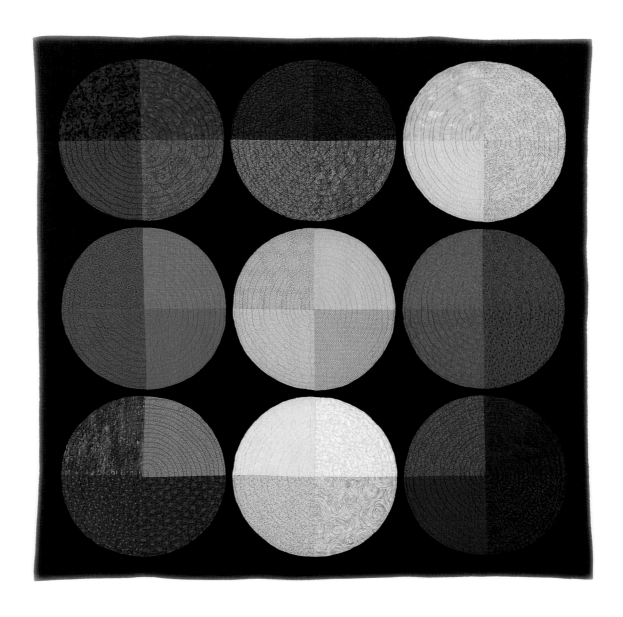

Jewel Box

40" × 40" (102 cm x 102 cm)
Bill Kerr and Weeks Ringle
of FunQuilts
2002

Cotton fabric and batting
Machine pieced and
machine quilted

Artists' Statement: "This quilt explores both hue and value. The value shift between the blues, reds, yellows, greens, and oranges on the edges and those in the center of the square make it appear that the black in the center of the quilt is lighter in value than that on the edges. Through these subtle value changes, part of the quilt appears to have a bright light shining on it while the rest appears in shadow. The simplicity of form allows the sophistication of the color work to shine through. This quilt was designed for sale as a limited series at the American Folk Art Museum in New York City."

PICK UP STICKS

48" × 72" (122 cm × 183 cm)
Bill Kerr and Weeks Ringle
of FunQuilts
2002

Cotton fabric and batting

Machine pieced and machine quilted

Artists' Statement: "Chaos within structure is the big idea here. Although the quilt is structured in a traditional block format, the sticks within each block were cut improvisationally to contrast with the grid of the blocks and be reminiscent of the random patterns created in a game of pick up sticks. Saturated colors across the color spectrum were chosen so the patterns of the sticks would read clearly. The creamy white field allows the colors and patterns to shine without distraction."

gallery

CRAYOLA ECLIPSE

72" × 86" (183 cm × 218 cm)
Ann Trotter
2000

Cotton fabric and batting
Paper pieced and
machine quilted

Artist's Statement: "In 1999 I started a portfolio of quilts that were created to complement professionally decorated rooms. This quilt was designed to hang in a contemporary room that features strong orange accents. I chose bright, vivid colors, transitioning from one color to another through pieced arcs."

HORIZON

40" × 48" (102 cm × 122 cm)
Bill Kerr and Weeks Ringle
of FunQuilts
1999
Cotton fabric and batting
Machine pieced and
machine quilted

Artists' Statement: "The Log Cabin block is one of the icons of American quiltmaking. The big idea here was to show how this block could be transformed into a contemporary pattern. The saturated blue contrasts with the rich reds of the background allow the graceful arc to be viewed without distraction. The centers of the blue Log Cabin squares are left red to imply a layering of the arc on top of the red field. Note also how the binding is pieced at the precise angle of the arc allowing the arc to continue off the edge of the quilt."

SKYSCRAPERS

32" × 32" (81 cm × 81 cm)
Sally Davey
2001

Cotton fabric and batting
Machine pieced,
machine appliquéd, and
machine quilted

Artist's Statement: "I am influenced by depth and light-play in quilts. I strive for clean, simple lines and a design that alludes to a building or idea. I like to play with color and its relationship to other colors. I have yet to meet a color combination that isn't successful as long as the proper design principles are applied. My style is ever evolving and, currently, I am doing architecturally inspired quilts. I hope it continues to evolve as I would like to experience it all for a long time to come."

MARY'S PINWHEEL

66" × 84" (168 cm × 213 cm)
Rebecca Rohrkaste
1989

*Cotton fabrics and cotton/
polyester batting*

*Machine pieced and
hand quilted*

Artist's Statement: "This tessellated pattern uses a wide variety of
fabrics, a full color spectrum, and a full, black to white range of value.
As in this quilt, I frequently favor a golden glow of color, sunlight, and
shadow, with the shadows (grays and cools) allowing the light to shine.
The literal golden yellow and golden browns here are obviously warm;
the medium violet though is both a complement, on the cool side of the
spectrum, and very much aglow."

FRAME OF MIND

two pieces, each 36" × 36"
(91 cm × 91 cm)
Rachel McCain
2002

Cotton fabric and batting
Machine pieced and
machine quilted

Artist's Statement: "In devising a color scheme for this quilt, my intent was to show the power of understatement. There is order and sophistication in the often-overlooked muted palette that can be absent from the chaos of our daily lives. The harmony of the quieter colors demonstrates that one does not always need to scream to be heard."

PINK LEMONADE

36" × 36" (91 cm × 91 cm)
Bill Kerr and Weeks Ringle
of FunQuilts
1999

Cotton fabric and batting
Machine pieced and
machine quilted

Artists' Statement: "The inspiration for *Pink Lemonade* came on a summer day when we noticed the beautiful coloration in a glass of pink lemonade. There was a perfect value fade from white where the ice was floating at the top of the glass to the deep pink at the bottom of the glass. To protect this delicate luminosity, no other hues were introduced that might have overwhelmed the paler pinks and whites."

Jewels of the Sea

61" × 78" (155 cm × 198 cm)
Chadidjah Alsegaf
1998

Cotton fabric and polyester batting

Machine appliquéd and machine quilted

Artist's Statement: "This quilt was inspired by the diversity of life in the ocean and jewels made from animal designs. It is a composition emphasizing texture and color, using about one thousand fish motifs that gave an unlimited flexibility in determining the design."

KINDNESS HAS NO BOUNDS

43" × 43" (109 cm × 109 cm)
Bonnie L. Connolly
2000

Cotton fabric and batting
Machine pieced by Bonnie
Connolly, machine quilted by
Heather Mulder

Artist's Statement: "This quilted wall hanging was begun in a class in Japan taught by Keiko Goke with an interpreter. As I had no supplies with me, generous Japanese quilters shared their fabric stashes. Even though language was an initial barrier, we communicated via the universal language of smiles, facial and hand gestures, and, of course, fabric. Upon returning home and auditioning several colors, I discovered that soft blue and medium to pale yellow set off the fractured heart in a pleasing aesthetic manner. The blue border is the use of the back side of a long-shelved fabric. The circular quilting was designed by me in phone and drawing collaboration with Heather Mulder, who machine quilted the wall hanging."

CROSSROADS

72" × 92" (183 cm × 234 cm)
Bill Kerr and Weeks Ringle
of FunQuilts
2001

Cotton fabric and batting
Machine pieced and
machine quilted

Artists' Statement: "Throughout the history of the world, towns have evolved at the intersections of roads. With towns came culture. This quilt celebrates what develops when travelers on different paths meet. Ochre earth tones represent the roads while rich jewel tones occur at the cross-roads, where culture occurs. These bright squares also recognize that art rarely happens in isolation but, rather, the artist is influenced by many people along the road."

WOMAN ON A JOURNEY

33" × 29" (84 cm × 74 cm)
Katharine Brainard
1993

Cotton fabric and batting
*Machine stitched and
hand stitched, machine
quilted, embroidery and
beading by hand*

Artist's Statement: "*Woman on a Journey* represents any woman seeking truth, authenticity, independence, an answer, a soul, a path. Color and image sources were ancient Egyptian and African art. The muted tones (reminiscent of vegetable dyes common before commercial dyes) convey a feeling of age. The gold rickrack and buttons communicate a sacred quality. The white and peach shell buttons provide not only accents, but a connection to the ocean, which relates to emotions. The energy shapes (color bursts, spirals) imply movement. The black background, framed by the lighter color in front, provides depth, suggesting that she is moving forward in time."

NORTHERN LIGHTS

75" × 98" (191 cm × 249 cm)
Bill Kerr and Weeks Ringle
of FunQuilts
1999

Cotton fabric and batting
Machine pieced and
machine quilted

Artists' Statement: *Northern Lights* is a study in luminosity, depth, and color. We carefully auditioned and arranged hundreds of fabrics so the warm reds, oranges, and yellows shine through the cooler grid of blues, greens, purples, and browns. Although hundreds of different printed fabrics were used in this quilt, the structure of the frame and the yellow-to-burgundy fade organize the quilt into one visual experience.

QUILT PROJECTS

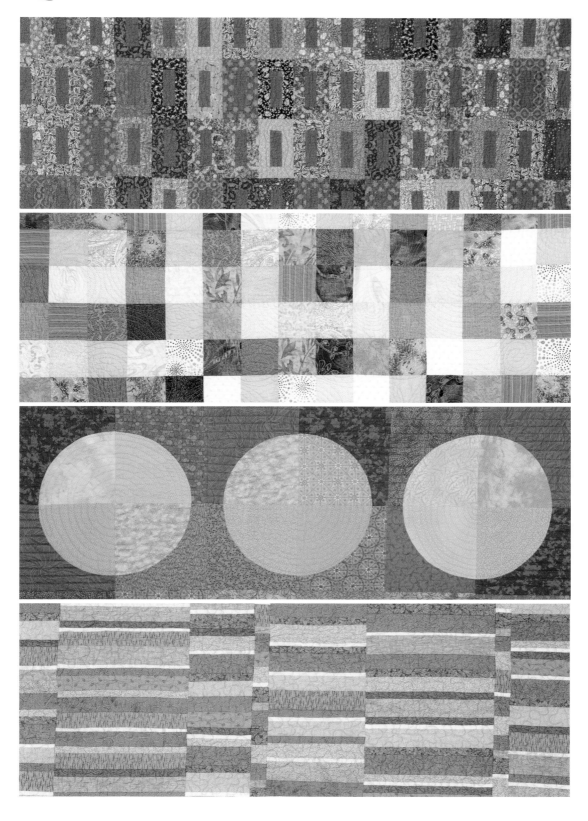

COLOR WORKBOOK

Students often ask us to explain the process we use to design a quilt and select colors for it. Often, the design begins with a Big Idea. We then design the pattern and make decisions about the fabric, the quilting, and the binding that will support the Big Idea. Occasionally, the process is more intuitive.

When a fabric or color combination catches our eye, we work backward to figure out why it is so captivating. What memory or sentiment does it evoke? It's caught our attention for some reason. When we figure out that reason, we've figured out the Big Idea.

Such was the case with our Zanzibar quilt, shown on the cover. We thought it would be useful to walk you through the thought process of this design because it demonstrates how following through on a hunch usually leads to something interesting, even if you don't have any idea where you are going when you're in the middle of it.

CASE STUDY: ZANZIBAR by Weeks Ringle

Design opportunities sometimes come when you least expect them. One day, I was walking through the warehouse of a fabric wholesaler, when I came upon a pile of multicolored remnants. Although I was not wild about each individual fabric there was something striking about the way someone had bundled them. I tried to figure out what it was about the combination that intrigued me. The first thing that popped into my mind was the dark, mysterious atmosphere of a coffee shop I had been to in Morocco when I was a teenager. Memories came back of cushions covered in patterned fabrics all over the floor, and patterned drapery covering the doorways and the windows to keep out the strong African sun. Among the remnants were dark multicolored fabrics with small-scale prints that looked very rich together. A second look suggested what a woman's closet might have looked like in the 1940s. Were these fabrics reproductions of old dress prints? Why were they so intriguing? If you wanted to use them in a quilt, how would you do it? I didn't have as clear a "Big Idea" as I would have liked by this time, but I knew it would come.

This is how the design process works sometimes. It begins with a series of thoughts that can seem unrelated, but there is an excitement that develops as your mind ponders the possibilities. The fact that something catches your eye is all that matters. Trying to consider and edit all the possibilities will take some time and patience, but that's when the real reward comes.

I ended up buying the whole bundle of remnants (even though I had just gone in to get a bolt of a simple blue print for a client...). Did I just pay a lot of money for a bunch of fabric that looks like I bought it at a flea market? Was Bill going to hate this stuff?

When I got back to the studio, Bill and I started to ponder the possibilities. To his credit, he reserved judgment about the palette until we had talked through the whole idea. We analyzed the fabric to figure out why they looked good together. They are all multi-colored prints with a similar level of desaturation (see color wheel). The prints are so small in scale that they don't compete with each other. Each fabric has many rich colors, but because the scale of each print is so small, from a distance you just see an overall hue with flecks of color.

**SWATCHES FROM
THE REMNANT BUNDLE**

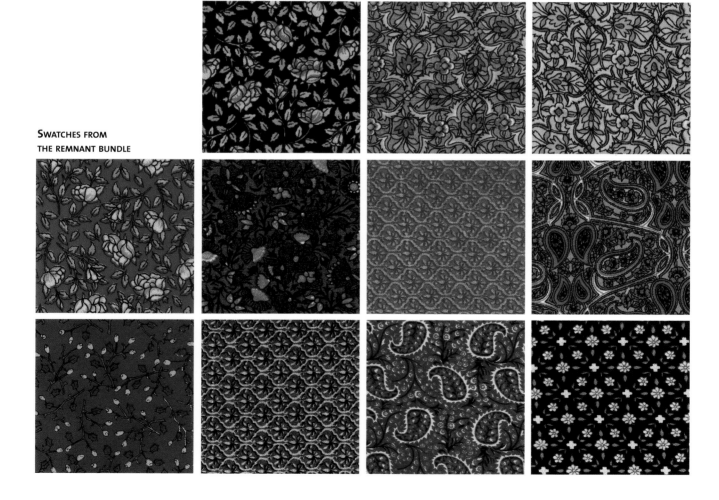

For more information on Color Theory, see page 8.

The pile of fabrics reminded us of the multicolored palette we chose for our more muted New Directions quilt (found on page 114 of the Gallery) four years earlier. While we often gravitate to a clean, "less is more" style for many of our quilts, when making New Directions we learned that sometimes, "more is more." By this we mean that if you were to randomly select six of these fabrics and make a quilt with them, it would be a disaster. It's only when you get twenty or thirty together that the palette really emerges. In the original pile of remnants at the warehouse, there were more than a dozen different fabrics and we knew that eleven would work well together. We knew that if we added another dozen, it would get even richer. So we combed through our stash to find other multi-colored, small-scale prints that might work.

We found fifteen more fabrics that did not necessarily match in hue, but did match in scale and saturation, and enhanced the original palette. The more we added, the better it looked. Despite the huge number of hues in the final palette, none stood out as too bright or too washed out.

FABRICS ADDED TO THE PALETTE

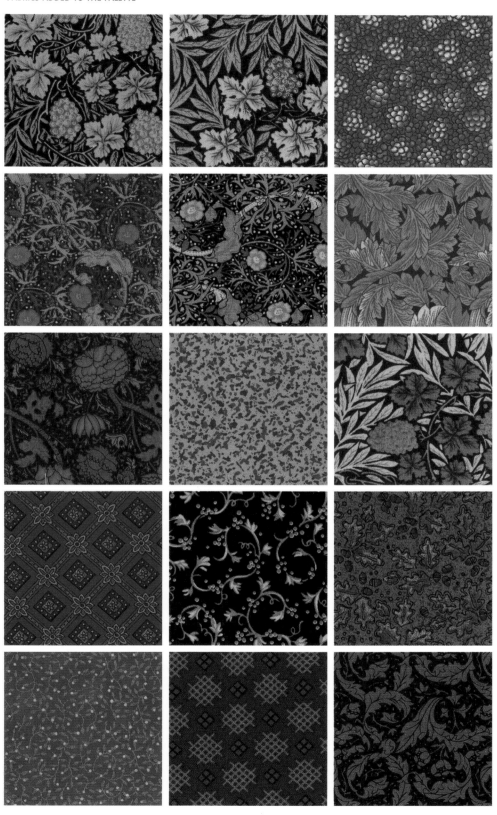

TOO BRIGHT

TOO LARGE-SCALE

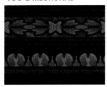

TOO DIRECTIONAL

TOO MONOCHROMATIC

BROWN CENTER ADDED TO PALETTE

We considered many more fabrics, which we later eliminated because they failed the ten-foot (3 m) rule: they popped too much when viewed with the other fabrics from a distance of ten feet (3 m). They popped for different reasons. Some were too bright. Some were eliminated because the scale of the pattern was too large, compared with the rest of the palette. Two were removed because they were too directional. Directional fabrics are a bad choice because they make the seams obvious. We pulled one fabric out because it was too monochromatic and looked flat among the multicolored fabrics. Another popped because it contained too much white.

Once we had assembled the palette, we realized the pattern for the quilt would have to be visually simple to accommodate so many colors and prints. We also referred back to New Directions, and realized that the repetition of a single element among a lot of unrelated fabrics unified it. Proportion became very important. If the block were too small, you wouldn't be able to see the rich texture of each print. If the block were too large, you'd miss the wonderful color collage that happens when you see all the fabrics together. Based on the scale of the actual fabrics, we came up with a size that would address both of these concerns.

We auditioned lots of different colors for the center of the block, but simultaneously said "Wow!" when we held up the brown. Suddenly, it looked like a spice rack. Then the "Big Idea" became clear. We visualized the spice markets of Zanzibar, with that warm, dark brown, the color of the native cloves. Once the Big Idea became clear, it was easier to make decisions about the quilting (something organic in form, not geometric) and binding (nothing too distracting from the complex color work). Part of the reason the brown worked is that it is a simple, monochromatic print that contrasts with the more complex multicolored prints. The calmness of the brown print provided some much needed breathing room for the other fabrics.

Once again, we were reminded that design is neither an easy process nor a predictable one. It took us several hours of pulling fabrics and discussing options before we knew if it was going to work. We weren't sure where we were going, but we were going back and forth between the intuitive side of design ("I like it") and the analytical side ("Why do I like it?"). In that back and forth process, solutions can often be found.

FABRIC SHOPPING GUIDE

Before You Leave for the Quilt Shop…

If you are like many of us who lead busy lives, a stop at the fabric store is often more rushed than you'd like, and you may have a child, a friend, or a spouse in tow. That means you sometimes have to make decisions more quickly than you'd prefer. Some students tell us that no matter how much time they have, the result is the same. They get into the shop, surrounded by 5,000 bolts of fabric, and they feel overwhelmed and begin to panic. A little time spent developing a strategy at home prior to setting foot in the fabric store is time well spent.

Say you've got a quilt in mind and you're trying to figure out which fabrics to use. Or maybe you've already bought a few yards of a fabric you love, but don't know what to do with it. Let's take it one step at a time and ask some general questions. You want to try to develop at least part of a "Big Idea" before you even start looking for fabric. Do this before you go to the store and it will make your design decisions much easier.

Who

For whom are you making the quilt? If you haven't bought the fabric yet and it's for your family, think about a word you would use to describe your family. If it's for someone else, think about what words you would use to describe the recipient. Is he or she warm or energetic or playful? Think about which colors might be appropriate for such a personality. Is there a particular color that you associate with them? Why?

Where

If it's for a friend, consider either openly or surreptitiously matching a swatch of paint or fabric of the room in which you think it might go. Think about how the quilt might be used. If there are pets in the house, know that nothing shows pet hair like black or white. If the quilt is likely to be handled by small children, darker colors might hide stains. The binding is going to get the dirtiest, so plan accordingly. If it's going to be washed a lot or handled by children, plan on quilting as densely as possible. Quilts that are stitched densely are more durable and look crisper than those with minimal stitching. If it's going on a wall, try to choose a color that contrasts with the color of the wall, either in hue, value, or both. A beige quilt on a beige wall may look flat, while another color such as white or blue might provide a fresh contrast.

Why

If you have already purchased some fabric or have a pattern in mind, figure out what it is about the pattern, the fabric, or the thought of making it that inspires you. Why does this fabric or pattern speak to you? It might be that you want to make it for a friend. Why do you want to make it? Is it a housewarming gift or a baby shower gift? Is it for your home? Take a minute to figure out what message you want it to convey.

Even a baby gift need not be made in predictable pinks or blues. One African-American student made a quilt for the baby she and her spouse were expecting that was cream, orange, and brown. These colors reminded her of the colors of the cotton and the soil that her ancestors worked amid in rural Georgia. It was a powerful reminder of her heritage that she wanted to convey to the baby. Her "Big Idea" was heritage and knowing your roots. Think about what the quilt might communicate to the recipient and choose a pattern and fabrics that support the message.

How

How important is this quilt to you? Be realistic, and plan the quilt according to how much it means to you and how much time you have available to finish it. Unfinished objects (UFOs as they are known among quilters) are depressing. They make us feel bad about the decisions we've made and reduce our enthusiasm for quilting. The best strategy for avoiding UFOs is to choose the pattern of the quilt, the size of the quilt, and the finishing of the quilt with some realistic understanding of how long it's going to take. As a rule of thumb, the more pieces, the more time it will take. Curved pieces require more pinning than quilts constructed with straight lines. Dense quilting can increase exponentially the amount of time it takes to make a quilt. We have seen some students use our longarm quilting machine to loosely quilt a queen-size bed cover in three hours, and others spend four hours densely quilting a table runner a fraction of the size. So, while size is an indicator, consider the number of pieces and the density of the quilting as being the main factors in determining how fast you'll be able to finish your quilt.

IN THE STORE

It's so easy to get overwhelmed in the quilt shop with all of those bolts of beautiful fabrics. Even those of us who work with fabric every day and have our own lines of fabric get in there and become totally unfocused. (See Weeks' story about the Zanzibar quilt on page 136.) Losing focus is not always a bad thing, but if you don't end up getting what you need or want, it can be frustrating. Here is a checklist that might make the experience a bit easier.

1. **Case the joint.** Look around to see where you might be able to stack your bolts for viewing from ten feet away. Obviously, you don't want to move any displays or inconvenience the shop. If possible, get as close to a natural light source (a door or a window) as possible. Figure out how the store is organized—is it by hue or by fabric collection? Are the new arrivals in a special section? Get a sense of what the shop carries so you don't overlook fabrics that are tucked away in an odd nook.

2. **Start pulling some bolts and stack them up.** Drape any swatches you've brought with you on top of them. If one fabric is the dominant fabric in the quilt, unwind enough of it so you can see it in greater proportion to the rest of the fabrics.

3. **Walk ten feet (3 m) away, and look at them.**

4. **Which fabrics pop out at you, and why?** Is it because one has white in it? If so, either add more prints with white in them or eliminate it from the palette. Are any of the fabrics more saturated than the others?

5. **Do any of the fabrics look muddy from a distance?** Are they too gray or too heavy in relation to the rest of the palette?

6. **Look for a backing fabric.** Place it next to the grouping.

7. **Look for a binding fabric.** Arrange it among the bolts so you can only see ½ " (1 cm) of it. This is the proportion in which you'll be seeing it when it becomes binding. Audition at least three different binding fabrics. You will be surprised at how a change in binding fabric can transform the palette.

8. **Choose your quilting thread.**

9. **Pay, thank the nice people at the quilt shop** (always treat employees at quilt shops with kindness— they know a ton, and you want to keep them around!), and get home to sew!

SOME BASIC QUILTMAKING TIPS

The four patterns from the FunQuilts studio in this book assume a basic knowledge of piecing, quilting, and binding. If you are new to quilting or wish to learn more about our approach to quiltmaking, you can learn the fundamentals of piecing, quilting, and binding in our book, *The Modern Quilt Workshop*. Whether you are an expert or novice quiltmaker, here are a few basic recommendations when making quilts:

- Use a $\frac{1}{4}$" (0.5 cm) seam allowance. This is a universal quilting standard when using cotton quilting fabrics. It is just wide enough that your seams will not pull apart, but not so much that they will be overly bulky.
- Prewash all fabrics in mild soap such as a tablespoon of Ivory Ultra dishwashing liquid or baby shampoo. Different fabrics shrink at different rates, and even high-quality fabrics occasionally bleed. You'll be handling the fabric a lot, so washing also reduces your exposure to chemical finishing agents.
- We recommend 100 percent cotton batting for its gentle drape and for the way it gets softer with age. We also love the way it shrinks just a bit, giving our quilts a lovely texture. Low-quality polyester batting can "beard" or poke through seams and fabric. The dimensions we give for the finished quilts are before shrinkage. If you are using cotton batting and plan to wash and machine dry your quilt, expect around 5 percent shrinkage.
- We iron all of our seams open rather than to the side when machine piecing and quilting. With hand quilting and hand piecing, seams are often ironed to the side, so that the quilting goes through all three layers and reinforces the seams. Many quiltmakers continue to press to the side even when machine quilting, but with the strength of machine stitching there is so little stress on the pieced seams that it is no longer an issue. We also prefer the way the quilt tops appear much more flat when seams are pressed open because it distributes the bulk of the seams evenly. If you plan to hand-piece or hand-quilt your quilt, iron your seams to the side.
- Be very cautious when working with a rotary cutter. Always close the cutter before setting it down. Never, ever set it down with an exposed blade, even for a moment.

Note: *The metric measurements used in the following quilt patterns are not straight conversions of the imperial sizes, but rather, are designed to result in a quilt that is similar in size, but allows for standard metric measurements.*

Zanzibar

SKILL LEVEL: simple |—|—②—|—| advanced
COLOR SKILL DEVELOPED: Unifying a broad palette of multicolored prints
SIZE: 51" x 75" (153 x 210 cm) napping quilt

Zanzibar's markets brim with fragrant spices. This island off the east coast of Africa is famous for its aromatic cloves, but is also a center of trade for cardamom, chilis, cinnamon, ginger, lemongrass, nutmeg, black pepper, sweet basil, turmeric, and vanilla. We captured this sensory richness in the blending of dozens of multicolored prints.

You can learn much more about how we selected the fabrics for this quilt in the case study on page 136. When selecting fabrics, avoid directional prints such as stripes. Choose a subtle print or a solid for the center rectangles to unify the quilt.

With its simple structure, this quilt is easily adaptable to other sizes, from small throws to wallhangings or queen-size quilts.

STRUCTURE:	Block size 3 ½" x 5 ½" (10 x 15 cm) cut size 3" x 5" (9 x 14 cm) finished size 255 blocks total 17 blocks across, 15 blocks down
FABRIC FOR CENTERS:	1 ¼ yards (1.25 m)
FABRIC FOR FRAMES:	¼ yard (25 cm) each of 24 fabrics
BACKING:	3 yards (3 m)
BINDING:	¾ yard (75 cm) for hand-sewn binding *or* ½ yard (50 cm) for machine-sewn binding

COLOR VARIATIONS

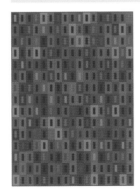 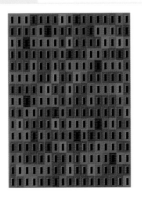  

figure 1

figure 2

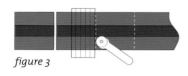

figure 3

figure 4

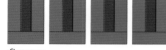

figure 5

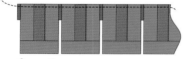

figure 6

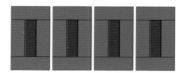

figure 7

figure 8

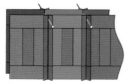

figure 9

INSTRUCTIONS

The basic block for this quilt has five pieces: a rectangular center and a frame made of four separate strips. (figure 1)

1. Cut twenty-four strips of the fabric for the centers 1 ½" x 40" (4 x 100 cm).

2. Cut four strips of one of the frame fabrics 1 ½" x 40" (4 x 100 cm).

3. Sew two of the four outer strips to the center strip, then iron the seams open. (figure 2)

4. Cut the fabric into eleven 3 ½" (9 cm) lengths. (figure 3)

5. Piece these one after another onto the third frame strip. (figure 4)

6. Iron seams open, then trim. (figure 5)

7. Piece these one after another onto the fourth and final frame strip. Iron seams open. (figure 6)

8. Iron seams open, then trim into finished blocks. (figure 7)

9. Repeat steps 2 through 8 using the remaining frame fabrics until you have at least 255 blocks. We usually make extras so that we can have more choices when we lay out the quilt.

10. Lay the quilt out on a design wall or on your floor. The quilt will be seventeen blocks across and fifteen blocks down. Make sure no two blocks of the same fabric are adjacent to each other. It'll probably take a lot of moving things around to get a composition you like. The goal is to distribute evenly the lightest and darkest or the most eye-catching fabrics so that your eye does not get "stuck" in one place when looking at the quilt. Back up at least ten feet (3 m) from the quilt to see the overall layout clearly. Once you are happy with the layout, number the rows so you can keep them in order. We use white or yellow schoolboard chalk to number because it washes out easily and is inexpensive. (figure 8)

11. Piece the blocks of each row together and iron the seams open.

12. Piece the rows together carefully, aligning the blocks by pinning through the seams. (figure 9)

13. Layer the top, batting, and backing; then quilt and bind.

Square Deal

SKILL LEVEL: simple ⊢—①—┼—┼—⊣ advanced
COLOR SKILL DEVELOPED: Making subtle value decisions
SIZE: 54" x 54" (135 x 135 cm)

Square Deal is a great quilt if you want to immerse yourself in a single color. You get to assemble a wide variety of fabrics of similar hues (all pinks or all greens, for example) but different values (lights and mediums or mediums and darks.) Begin by combing through your stash, or by going to the quilt shop and sorting fabrics into two piles by value. You could choose to make the two piles distinctly different, with the lights being far lighter than the darks. We selected fabrics that sometimes blur the line, making the pattern of the quilt more subtle.

Fabrics with high-value contrast prints may be difficult to use. Tone-on-tone fabrics will lend themselves better to the subtle value differences needed to make this quilt work.

STRUCTURE:	Square size: 3 ½" x 3 ½" (8.5 x 8.5 cm) cut size 3" x 3" (7.5 x 7.5 cm) finished size 18 squares across, 18 squares down 324 squares total 168 light squares 156 dark squares
FABRIC FOR CENTERS:	minimum of 8 fabrics, ¼ yard (25 cm) each
FABRIC FOR FRAMES:	minimum of 8 fabrics, ¼ yard (25 cm) each
BACKING:	3 ½ yards (3.5 m)
BINDING:	¾ yard (75 cm) for hand-sewn binding *or* ½ yard (50 cm) for machine-sewn binding

COLOR VARIATIONS

 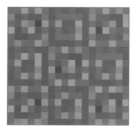  

INSTRUCTIONS

1. Cut 168 squares of the light fabrics. You can simplify the cutting by starting with a 3 ½" (8.5 cm) strip the width of the fabric, then trim that into 11 squares. (figure 1)

2. Randomly piece together the light fabrics into eighty-four pairs, then iron the seams open. (figure 2)

3. Cut 156 squares of the dark fabrics.

4. Randomly piece together the dark fabrics into seventy-eight pairs, then iron the seams open.

5. Lay out these pairs to form the entire quilt. Once you are happy with the layout, number the pairs so you can keep them in order. We use white or yellow schoolboard chalk to number because it washes out easily and is inexpensive. (figure 3)

6. Piece the pairs together, ironing seams open as you go. You can align the squares by pinning through the seams. (figure 4)

7. Layer the top, batting, and backing; then quilt and bind.

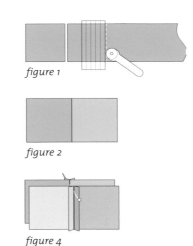

figure 1

figure 2

figure 4

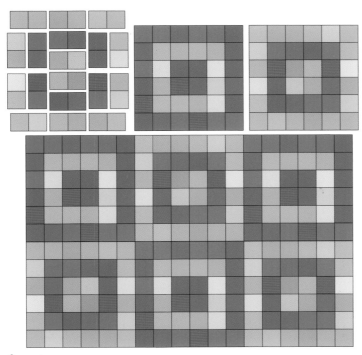

figure 3

Mod

SKILL LEVEL: simple ├──┼──③──┼──┤ advanced

COLOR SKILL DEVELOPED: Working with saturated colors

SIZE: 41" x 41" (107 x 107 cm)

Mod is not a shy quilt. It makes a strong color statement with its bold geometry and large expanses of fabric. While the daring color combination shown here announces itself loudly, you could recolor the quilt with a selection of gentle blues and greens or make it in graphic reds, whites, and blacks. The ease of piecing the large diameter circles will amaze those who have circle phobia.

When selecting fabric, look for monochromatic tone-on-tone prints which read as solids from a distance. Avoid strongly directional prints such as stripes, and steer clear of high-contrast prints or ones with large-scale motifs.

STRUCTURE:	36 blocks of three sizes with inset quarter circles
FABRIC FOR CENTER PIECES:	5 or more fabrics, ¼ yard (25 cm) each
FABRIC FOR OUTER PIECES:	5 fabrics, ½ yard (50 cm) each
FABRIC FOR CIRCLES:	6 or more fabrics, ¼ yard (25 cm) each
BACKING:	1 ¼ yards (1.25 m)
BINDING:	½ yard (50 cm)

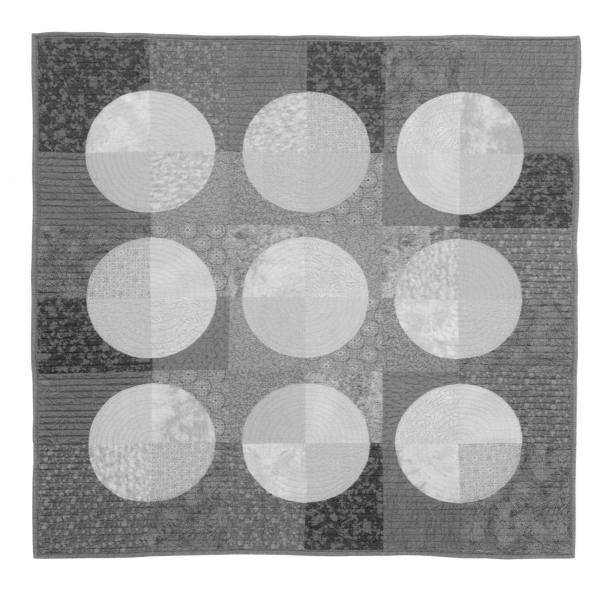

COLOR VARIATIONS

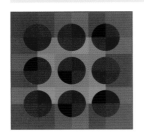 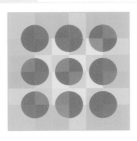  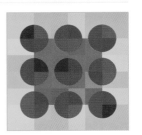

INSTRUCTIONS

1. Trace pattern A and pattern B (found on page 157) onto pattern plastic, or photocopy onto card stock. Label your patterns.

2. Using pattern A, cut fourty-eight quarter circles from your circle (orange) fabrics.

3. The outer (purple) blocks come in two sizes: square corners and rectangular interior pieces. From different fabrics, cut the four corner squares 9 ½" x 9 ½" (24 x 24 cm). Next, cut the sixteen interior rectangles 9 ½" x 6 ¼" (24 x 16 cm). (figure 1)

4. Cut sixteen squares of the inner (fuchsia) fabrics 6 ¼" x 6 ¼" (16 x 16 cm).

5. Align template B to the corner of each square and rectangle, and cut out. (figure 2)

6. Lay out the entire quilt. Once you are happy with the layout, number the pieces so that you can keep them in order. We use white or yellow schoolboard chalk to number because it washes out easily and is inexpensive.

7. Piece quarter circles into blocks one set at a time. (figure 3)

8. Find the centers of the two pieces in each set by folding them in half. Placing right sides together, align them at the center creases and pin at number 1. Next, pin the edges at numbers 2 and 3. Insert final pins at the midway points, numbers 4 and 5. You can find these midway points by folding the edges to the center and creasing. (figure 4)

9. Sew pieces together slowly, maintaining a ¼" (0.5 cm) seam allowance. Keep the quarter circle flat down on the machine and the square on top. If you try to sew it with the circle on top, you will get puckers and tucks. The curves are large, so you don't need to notch them before ironing the seams open on the back. Iron the finished block again on the front. (figure 5)

10. Assemble blocks into rows, pinning through seams to ensure alignment. (figure 6)

11. Sew together the rows, pinning through seams to ensure alignment. (figure 7)

12. Layer the top, batting, and backing; then quilt and bind.

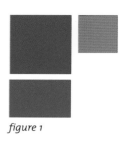

figure 1

figure 2

figure 3   *figure 4*

figure 5   *figure 6*

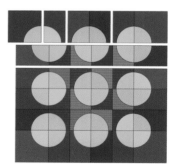

figure 7

Out of Line

SKILL LEVEL: simple ├───┼───┼───┤⑤ advanced
COLOR SKILL DEVELOPED: Working with proportions of color
SIZE: 72" x 48" (182 x 122 cm)

This quilt was inspired by textiles that Weeks inherited from a Great Aunt who traveled the world in the 1940s. No one is quite sure of the origin of the richly colored, striped textiles, but their design is timeless. When stacked, the group of striped textiles looked so wonderful together that we wanted to capture the effect in a design. The weavers of the original pieces understood that some colors are stronger than others and need to be seen in smaller amounts so as not to overwhelm the more understated colors.

When assembling your palette, step away from the pile and see which color is the boldest. Use that in smaller amounts. Likewise, the color that is the most subdued, relative to the rest of the palette, can be used in larger amounts. Consider a complimentary color for the smallest stripe. A small amount of a contrasting color can transform a quilt. Avoid using the contrasting color for the binding, though, which would be an unwelcome distraction from the design of the quilt.

STRUCTURE:	Improvisationally pieced bands of varying sizes
FABRIC:	3 or more blue fabrics totaling 2 yards (2 m) 3 or more red fabrics totaling 2 yards (2 m) 3 or more green fabrics totaling 1 ½ yards (1.5 m) 3 or more yellow fabrics totaling 1 yard (1 m)
BACKING:	3 ½ yards (3.5 m)
BINDING:	¾ yard (75 cm) for hand-sewn binding *or* ½ yard (50 cm) for machine-sewn binding

STRIP SIZE	YELLOWS	BLUES	REDS	GREENS
¾" (2 cm)	30	–	–	–
1" (2.5 cm)	–	15	20	10
1 ½" (4 cm)	–	15	15	15
1 ¾" (4.5 cm)	–	15	10	10

quilt projects

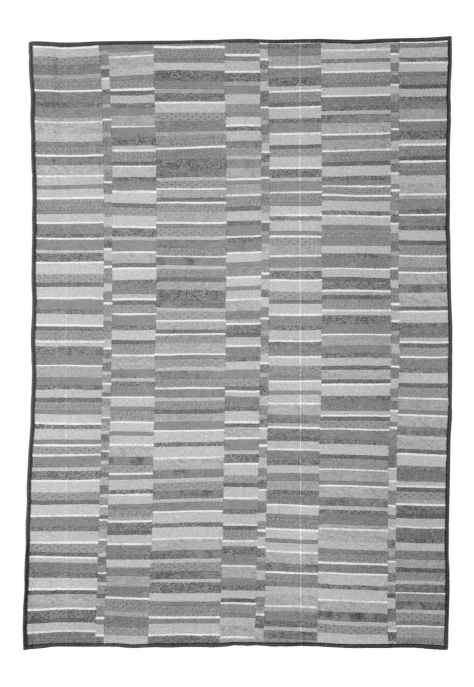

COLOR VARIATIONS

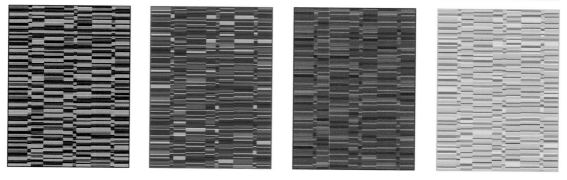

INSTRUCTIONS

1. Cut the required number of strips of the blue, red, green, and yellow fabrics according to the chart on page 153. Cut each strip the full width of the fabrics from selvedge to selvedge (about 42" [107 cm]).

2. Sew ten strips together in random order, alternating the widths of the bands as you go. Include just two yellow strips in each group of ten. Keep one end of the strips in the group relatively flush. (figure 1)

3. Repeat step 2 eleven more times until you have twelve sets of striped bands. Iron all the seams open.

4. Cut eight of the bands into six segments: one 4 ½" (11.5 cm) segment, one 5 ½" (14 cm) segment, two 6 ½" (16.5 cm) segments, and two 8 ½" (21.5 cm) segments. You'll probably have some bits left over which you can save and reuse later for a 1 ½" (4 cm) segment. (figure 2)

5. From the remaining three bands, cut ten more 8 ½" (21.5 cm) segments. You'll have some fabric left over. (figure 3)

6. Using the leftover ends from all the strips, cut enough 1 ½" (4 cm) segments so that you can assemble three 75" (190 cm) long strips. (figure 4)

7. Lay out the segments into ten columns, rotating and moving strip segments to avoid obvious patterns. The sequence of the strip widths is: 8 ½", 1 ½", 5 ½", 8 ½", 4 ½", 1 ½", 6 ½", 8 ½", 1 ½", 6 ½" (21.5 cm, 4 cm, 14 cm, 21.5 cm, 11.5 cm, 4 cm, 16.5 cm, 21.5 cm, 4 cm, 16.5 cm). Once you are happy with the layout, number the segments so you can keep them in order. We use white or yellow schoolboard chalk to number because it washes out easily and is inexpensive. Sew the segments together, ironing seams open, to form columns 72" (1.82 m) long. (figure 5)

8. Sew the columns together.

9. Layer the top, batting, and backing, then quilt and bind.

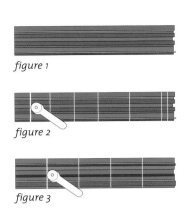

figure 1

figure 2

figure 3

figure 4

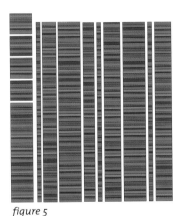

figure 5

COLOR PLANNER

Copy this sheet, fold in half, and staple or glue to form an envelope. Fill with fabric swatches you'd like to work with, or staple them here to the edge so that you have them in the shop with you.

IN THE STORE

Ask yourself the following questions:

- Are the fabrics organized by color, collection, or both?
- Is there a natural light source?
- Where is the brightest light?

Locate a space (near a natural light source if possible) where you can stack your bolts and view them from ten feet (3 m) away without disturbing displays.

When auditioning fabrics for the binding, stack the bolts so you can only see 1/2" (0.5 cm) of the fabric, with a larger proportion of the fabrics that will appear on the front and back.

NOTIONS YOU NEED:

thread
batting
rotary blades
pins
needles
notions
fabric markers
rulers
other

NOTES:

---

cm 1 2 3 4 5 6 7 8 9 10 11 12

inches 1 2 3 4 5

fold

BEFORE YOU GO

Name of Project:

Finished size of project:

My Big Idea is:

I need a total of:

_____ yards/meters of _____ fabrics for the quilt top

_____ yards/meters of _____ fabrics for the back

_____ yards/meters of _____ fabric for binding

AMOUNT	COLOR	DESCRIBE SHADE/PATTERN
_____	red	
_____	orange	
_____	yellow	
_____	green	
_____	blue	
_____	purple	
_____	brown	
_____	gray	
_____	black	
_____	white	
_____	multicolor	
_____	other	

PATTERNS

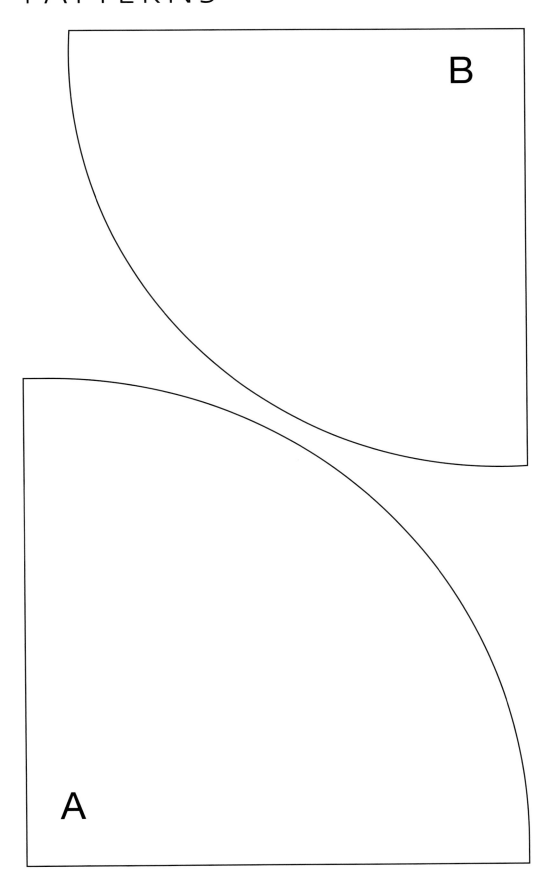

CONTRIBUTORS

Chadidjah Alsegaf
Bethesda, Maryland
(34, 134)

Katharine Brainard
krbrainard@aol.com
www.katharinebrainard.com
(94, 137)

Bonnie Connolly
Kenosha, Wisconsin
(135)

Sally Davey
(130)

Judy Hasheider
Sauk City, Wisconsin
(112)

Catherine Kleeman
Baltimore, Maryland
cathy@cathyquilts.com
www.cathyquilts.com
(40)

Rachel McClain
Chicago, Illinois
(132)

Jan Myers-Newbury
Pittsburgh, Pennsylvania
samanjan@bellatlantic.net
(82, 125)

Paula Nadelstern
Bronx, New York
www.paulanadelstern.com
(100, 126)

Sushma Patel-Bould
East Palo Alto, California
www.sushmaquilts.com
(58)

Rebecca Rohrkaste
Berkeley, California
(52, 131)

Jane Sassaman
Chicago, Illinois
www.janesassaman.com
(88)

Gloria Spaete
Columbus, Wisconsin
pspaete@internetwis.com
(70, 121)

Heather Waldron Tewell
Anacortes, Washington
(46, 120)

Ann Trotter
Green Bay, Wisconsin
atrots@yahoo.com
(64, 124)

Angie Woolman
Albany, California
adwool@pacbell.net
(106, 128)

RESOURCES

The following listings are just a few of many great resources for inspiration, scholarship, and supplies.

For color inspiration, we suggest you look not only at great quilts, but at great examples of color in art, architecture, sculpture, graphic design, landscape architecture, and nature. In addition to the resources in your public library and nearby museums, there are inspirational examples of color in both the natural and man-made world all around you.

The American Craft Museum
www.americancraftmuseum.org
40 W. 53rd Street
New York, NY 10019
212.956.3535
Exhibitions of contemporary crafts including quilts.

The American Folk Art Museum
www.folkartmuseum.org
45 W. 53rd Street
New York, NY 10019
212.265.1040
A museum featuring the work of self-taught American artists. The museum hosts or curates quilt exhibits and has many important quilts in its collection.

The American Quilter's Society
www.aqsquilt.com
P.O. Box 3290
Paducah, KY 42002
AQS is famous for its enormous annual quilt show in Paducah, Kentucky, its quilt museum, and its publications.

The Dairy Barn Cultural Arts Center
www.dairybarn.org
8000 Dairy Lane
Athens, OH 45701
740.592.4981
The Dairy Barn organizes "Quilt National," a biennial exhibit of art quilts. It also sponsors a wide range of workshops and classes in quilting and other arts.

The International Quilt Study Center
Department of Textiles, Clothing, & Design
University of Nebraska-Lincoln
234 Home Economics Building
Lincoln, NE 68583-0802
The University of Nebraska-Lincoln is home of The International Quilt Study Center. It is the only institution that offers a graduate program in textile history and textile design with an emphasis in quilt studies. The IQSC has the country's largest public collection of quilts (more than 1,200) and extensive resources for quilt and textile scholarship.

The Quilter's Travel Companion
Available through quilt shops or through:
Chalet Publishing
32 Grand Avenue
Manitou Springs, CO 80829
A guidebook to more than 2,000 quilting shops across North America. Organized by state and region, it also includes contact information for hundreds of regional quilting guilds.

Quilts, Incorporated
www.quilts.com
7660 Woodway, Suite 550
Houston, TX 77063
713.781.6864
Quilts, Inc., is the parent company of three large, consumer quilt shows and the largest quilting trade show in the United States.

The San Jose Museum of Quilts and Textiles
www.sjquiltmuseum.org
110 Paseo de San Antonio
San Jose, CA 95112-3639
408.971.0323
This museum is dedicated to both traditional and contemporary quilts and offers workshops and lectures.

About the Authors

Weeks Ringle and Bill Kerr are professional quiltmakers and founders of FunQuilts, a contemporary quilt design studio in Oak Park, Illinois. Their work has been featured in more than 40 publications including *O: The Oprah Magazine*, *Metropolitan Home*, *Country Living*, the *New York Times*, and *Interior Design*. They have written about color and design for *American Patchwork & Quilting* and *Quilts Japan*. They also design fabrics for FreeSpirit, which are available internationally. Weeks and Bill live with their daughter in Oak Park, Illinois.

Acknowledgments

We are grateful to our contributors for providing us with a diverse and wonderful collection of quilts from which to learn. For their help in cutting and piecing some of the quilts in this book, we thank Deanna Harris and Mary Phemister. Our students continue to amaze and inspire us and we thank them.

We would like to thank Mary Ann Hall and everyone at Quarry Books for their interest in quilts and their dedication to design and publishing excellence.

Photography Credits

Hadi Alsegaf, Jewels of the Sea, page 130; Old China, page 30

Karen Bell, Kaleidoscopic XVII: Caribbean Blues, page 122; Kaleidoscopic XXI: The Thank Your Lucky Star Memorial Quilt, page 96

Brian Blauser Best, Century Plant, page 84; Ground Cover I, page 115

Bobbie Bush, page 5

Charles Crust, Of Current and Tide, page 116; Sunlight on Flowers, page 42

Sam Newbury, Forest Floor, page 121; Agape, page 78

Gary Putnam, Divorce Quilt, page 90

Kevin Thomas, pages 8, 12, 14, 36, 42, 54, 60, 66, 108, 114, 117, 118, 119, 120, 123, 126, 128, 129, 131, 134